After his first child became a toddler, Justin Coulson realised he wasn't the dad he wanted to be. To learn more about parenting, he quit a successful radio broadcasting career and started studying, eventually completing a PhD in Positive Psychology and Parenting. Justin is an honorary fellow at the Centre for Positive Psychology at the University of Melbourne.

Justin lives with his wife and six daughters in Brisbane, Queensland, and travels Australia constantly, giving talks to parents, teachers and professionals. He is the author of *21 Days to a Happier Family* and *9 Ways to a Resilient Child*.

Visit www.happyfamilies.com.au

10 Things
Every Parent
Needs to Know

Dr Justin Coulson, PHD

ABC
BOOKS

Author's note

In the stories shared in this book, names and other details have been altered to protect the privacy of individuals, with the exceptions of those when permission was granted to use real names and examples drawn from my own family.

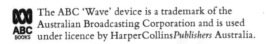 The ABC 'Wave' device is a trademark of the Australian Broadcasting Corporation and is used under licence by HarperCollins*Publishers* Australia.

First published in Australia in 2018
by HarperCollins*Publishers* Australia Pty Limited
ABN 36 009 913 517
harpercollins.com.au

HarperCollins*Publishers*
Level 13, 201 Elizabeth Street, Sydney NSW 2000, Australia
Unit D1, 63 Apollo Drive, Rosedale, Auckland 0632, New Zealand
A 53, Sector 57, Noida, UP, India
1 London Bridge Street, London, SE1 9GF, United Kingdom
Bay Adelaide Centre, East Tower, 22 Adelaide Street West, 41st floor, Toronto,
   Ontario M5H 4E3, Canada
195 Broadway, New York NY 10007, USA

A catalogue record for this book is available
from the National Library of Australia

ISBN: 978 0 7333 3872 4 (paperback)
ISBN: 978 1 4607 0899 6 (ebook : epub)

Cover design by Hazel Lam, HarperCollins Design Studio
Cover image by Lea Csontos /stocksy.com /633982
Internal design by Darren Holt, HarperCollins Design Studio
Typeset in Adobe Garamond Pro by Kirby Jones
Printed and bound by CPI Group (UK) Ltd, Croydon, CR0 4YY

For every parent who has
wanted to be better

Contents

Contents

Foreword

Parenting today in our consumer-driven, fast-paced digital world has become clouded with stress and confusion. As a parenting author and educator, I am aware of the things that worry parents – from taming toddler tantrums to 'how do I get my kids to sleep' and 'is this normal?'.

In a way, there is too much information, often simply a click away, which means parents can become even more confused when they are looking for guidance to navigate common parenting dilemmas. Then there's the massive footprint of social media, where images of 'perfect' family moments abound. In real life, there is no 'perfect' – and good enough, imperfect parenting can still raise children into compassionate, effective adults who live meaningful lives. I am a proud (often imperfect) mum to four adult sons who are doing great as they now become caring husbands and devoted dads.

In *10 Things Every Parent Needs to Know*, Dr Justin Coulson explores some of the common areas of concern for parents everywhere. He does this in his unique, reassuring way by owning his own less-than-perfect parenting experiences, as well as exploring what research brings to the table in terms of solutions.

Justin captures parenting so well. From the disaster moments when we feel like inadequate failures, to the moments of exquisite delight when our hearts could break open with the love pulsing through them.

In a way, every parent is making it up as they go along and hoping they don't muck up their kids. I also firmly believe every parent is doing the best they can with what they've got. There are times that we may seek more wisdom because we feel we could do better. When we find well-informed parenting educators who can advise us without making us feel worse, that's fabulous. Justin is one of those passionate educators.

This book will help parents feel more confident in the daily and weekly decisions they make in their homes while learning what matters most in children's lives. Justin and I share a passion for helping parents enjoy this unpredictable journey more — by focusing on loving our children ferociously and unconditionally. This means consciously making memories that matter and actively seeking joy and laughter because homes in which these are a priority will be safer, happier homes for everyone.

Maggie Dent
Author and parenting and resilience specialist

Introduction

Confession: I struggle as a parent.

The day I had to tell one of my young children to take her feet off her food, I knew this was going to be tougher than I had imagined.

As I'm the 'parenting expert', you probably want some assurance that my kids are perfect. They're not. They're kids, not robots.

And I know that you probably hoped I had my stuff together. You need me to know what I'm talking about. Well … I do, but it's still hard to get it right all the time. Sometimes it's hard to get it right at all. If you're a parent, you know what I mean.

Before Kylie and I had children, I thought it would be easy enough to have kids. Be clear. Be consistent. Be 'the parent'. How hard could it be? On more than one occasion I may have seen parents struggling with their children and made suggestions to them on how they might do it better. My input earned me some stares that looked hostile. Even violent! Those parents never *actually* hit me when I shared my ideas on how they could parent better, but … if looks could kill! I'm pretty sure that there were times they really came close!

And then the day arrived. Kylie and I decided we no longer wanted to sleep in, disappear for a weekend whenever we felt like it, or enjoy quiet evenings in cafés or restaurants. We didn't want to live in a clean house any more. And we had tired of being able to simply get in the car and go somewhere spontaneously just for the fun of it. We wanted children! We wanted it to take 45 minutes to get everyone into the car, only to have to stop three minutes into the trip because someone wanted to go to the toilet! We wanted to share our bed with a contortionist who believed that a queen-sized mattress was only big enough for one person, aged two and a bit. We wanted to be *wanted* by someone so badly that we would hear our names screamed into our ears over a hundred times before 7 am.

When our firstborn was three I discovered that parenting is like eating with chopsticks: it looks pretty simple until you try, but if you're not careful, it's easy to fail and make a terrible mess – especially as a beginner.

The struggle was real. It was my inability to deal with my firstborn behaving like a 'threenager' that led to me quitting a successful career as a radio announcer and going to university for nearly a decade to learn how to dad better. A psychology degree and a PhD, plus some years lecturing and researching at university, gave me the credentials. Having six children of our own gave me the experience. And it worked. For a while. But all the good rules about parenting can still leave us feeling stuck. Like I said, kids aren't robots. (Neither are parents.) And consistency alone can't be the answer.

Parenting is tough. And it's easy to get things wrong. I was reminded of this fact following a conflict between one of my daughters and me. Kylie pointed out that I had behaved like a child in responding to my daughter's challenging behaviour – and *not* like a grown-up (and especially not like a parenting expert).

Like so many parents, I was over-stretched, over-worked, and over-tired. A child had pushed my buttons. I had over-reacted to my daughter's transgression and, in doing so, I'd acted like I'd forgotten most of the stuff I share with thousands and thousands of people day in and day out. Kylie was right. I *had* behaved like a child. A badly behaved child.

I hung my head in shame for a couple of days. And honestly, what parent hasn't? We all mess it up. We all say the wrong words, get angry or frustrated, or allow our worry and fear for our children to spew out of us in unhelpful ways. It can be easy to forget that our children are people, too. They need to make choices, to learn and to grow. It is even easier to forget that our children's choices can promote *our* growth, too. (More on that later ...)

But out of that incident came the conviction that I *had* to write this book. If 'the expert' is having a rough go of it, how is everyone else feeling? Deep down I knew I had to write this book *because of incidents like that.* Stuff like this – and unfortunately worse – happens in homes all over the place, all the time.

So ... we *all* mess up (to varying degrees). I do it. You do it. It's called being a parent.

Here's something I've noticed though. Every parent I talk to wants to do better. We want to have fewer awful moments. We know we *can* respond with more patience, show greater compassion and listen more intently. And we beat ourselves up when we fail to live up to what we expect of ourselves. Like this mum, who emailed me:

> Hi Justin,
>
> I am the epitome of everything you disagree with as a parent. I smack. I yell. I put kids in time out. I have no patience – especially with my son.
>
> I hate it. I hate me as a mum. I know I am failing my children and I just can't stop. I lose my temper and what is worse, I have to fight the feeling of wanting to actually smack so hard that I want to hurt my son. To teach him a lesson. I know you're right and I'm wrong. I need help. I have read your articles and what you say resonates so much with me. I want to change. I want to be a better mum.

Have you ever said the same things to yourself?

> 'I hate who I've become. I hate the way I'm treating my kids. I hate that I can't do this. They deserve more than me. I want to be better. They need me to be better!'

I have. I know how it feels. It's an awful pain in my heart.

When you listen to what is deep inside you, perhaps you can hear the same plea. We want to do the very best for our children. We hate it when we fail to live up to our ideals.

When we get it wrong, it's easy to blame the kids. 'It's their fault I'm behaving like this. If they'd just do as they were *asked*!'

But if we're mature and thoughtful about it, we realise that being a great parent is not really so much about the children. It's far more about *us*. It's about how *we* deal with things in positive and constructive ways. We say the children are driving us mad – and sometimes they are. But often it's only partly their behaviour that is upsetting. What really gets us deep down is the way *we* act towards *them*!

The desperation that the mum on the previous page felt is vital. Maybe you have felt it too. There's an important difference between feeling desperate and feeling discouraged. Feeling *discouraged* makes us feel lousy about ourselves. We feel hopeless and helpless. Then we treat the kids badly, which reminds us of how hopeless we are, and then we fall into deeper discouragement.

Feeling *desperate* and admitting it – well that helps us realise we can't do it ourselves, and so we look to other sources to guide us. This is where growth and learning occur. Desperation acknowledged is a sure sign of soon-to-arrive success! It shows that despite nothing working, we are willing to keep trying. We have hope and desire. We just need a pathway to follow. Or an instruction manual.

They're not born with an instruction manual

It's the most overused cliché in the parenting world, but it reflects a critical reality. None of us is really prepared for the task at hand. No one teaches us how to parent. Trial and error is the default. Our children don't come with an instruction manual. *They are the manual.* But many of us find it challenging to read children-ese. Instead, we learn parenting from our parents and the people around us. We watch, judge, evaluate, try ideas out and make it up as we go along.

But as our children mature, the terrain keeps shifting. Our children are continually developing. And what worked or was permissible in the 1980s or the 1990s may not work today. Now we have new challenges, new fears and new opportunities. In this book, I describe ten key requirements for successful, joyous parenting – tenets that will help us guide our children to live successful lives. I'd go so far as to say these are the ten things every parent needs to know to raise their children in positive ways. They are ten ways life can be easier for you – so you don't have to keep making things up to get through.

These ten things parents need to know may or may not be new to you. But you'll find positive parenting solutions that will reinforce what you know works, and spark some great new ideas to strengthen your parenting and your family. This book is written to help you feel better about – and do better in – your parenting. I believe that in the process, you'll make your family happier.

I've heard it said that no other success can compensate for failure in the home.

The work we do as parents is our most important work. It will probably impact the world more than anything else we do. And it will impact the lives of our children, grandchildren and great-grandchildren in inescapable ways. How we raise our children casts a long shadow over the rest of our lives – and theirs.

A final note before we launch into the book. I've written this book to make *you* the parenting expert in your family. The truth is that while I know a bunch of useful stuff every parent needs to understand, I believe you probably already know most of it, even if you can't yet put it into words. So I'm going to ask you questions, challenge you and get you thinking about ways that you can lean on *your* expertise and experience in your home. I'll make suggestions and give you ideas. But be prepared for me to ask you to reflect on and evaluate the times you've done it just right – many times throughout the book. *Your successful experiences will be your most powerful and positive guides.*

Raising children can be – should be – one of the most delightful, rewarding, joyful aspects of our lives. This book will help you experience it that way.

Parenting on the same page

A couple were in a busy shopping centre just after Christmas. The wife was talking with her husband – or so she thought. She looked around and noticed he was missing. How long had he been gone?

She called his mobile phone and asked, 'Where are you?' She gave him a stern reminder: 'You know we have lots to do!'

He responded, 'I know. Sorry. I just had to do something. Do you recall the jewellers we went into about ten years ago? You fell in love with that diamond necklace? I couldn't afford it, and I said that one day I would get it for you?'

The wife began to cry as she remembered the day. All choked up and full of expectation she whispered into the phone, 'Yes, I do remember that shop.'

'Well, I'm in the bike shop next door.'

If we are fortunate enough to be in a relationship, chances are that we really, *really* love our partner*. We want to have great relationships and a happy family. One of the biggest challenges in relationships is

---

* There is a list of resources at the end of the book
   if this description does not apply to you right now.

that we tend to see things – and think about things – very differently. What seems fair and reasonable to one parent/partner may seem harsh to another. What makes perfect sense to one parent is way too soft and permissive to the other. Parenting polarises opinion, even within a family. And what start out as small, manageable differences in opinion become gaping chasms as we defend our opinions.

The number one parenting question

The most consistent question I hear about parenting actually has nothing to do with the children. Instead, it's about 'same-page parenting'. I get so many emails and Facebook messages where someone will explain that they love the parenting strategies I share, but their partners won't get on board. Usually it will be Mum who will explain that she wants to be warm and nurturing and Dad wants to teach the children with tough love. Some fathers ask for help in changing their partners' ways. A mum will explain she is trying to be nurturing but her husband is easily angered, and all too often aggressive towards the children. Dad is worried that Mum adopts a 'my way or the highway' approach to childrearing. 'It's my house, my rules.'

One mum said to me, 'It's ridiculous that I share a bed with this guy. I've had children with him because it's what *we* wanted. But now we've got them, we don't agree on anything about how to raise them!'

The disagreements start early. Baby sleep is the one I've heard complained about more often than most.

Mum: The baby's crying again. Why won't she sleep?

Dad: She's going to have to learn that we're not going to pick her up every time she screams. It's been going on for an hour now. We're going to have to let her cry it out. She'll go to sleep eventually. My sister said it only took three nights and bedtime was easy after that.

Mum: Your sister went through hell. And it was weeks. And I don't want my baby to scream herself to sleep every night. I need to pick her up.

Dad: I hate it as much as you but we've got to do something. I think we need to just let her cry. Neither of us wants this, but this is what I reckon. I'm going to go and sit in the car so I don't have to listen to it.

Mum: She's only a baby. I can't do this.

Sometimes conflict erupts because of desperation for a solution. It may be exhaustion. Other times one parent is sure they're right and the other is wrong. Once the children are older, the pages turn, but we're still on different pages.

Dad: They'll be fine. It's less dangerous than it looks.

Mum: That tree is so high. How are they going to get down?

Dad: Don't worry about it. Didn't you ever climb trees when you were a kid? This is what a real childhood's all about!

Mum: Does it have to be *ten* metres up in the air?

Or this one:

Dad: Kids, Mum and I cook healthy meals for you to eat. We don't cook this stuff for you to turn your noses up at it. So you're gonna sit there and eat it, or you'll have it for breakfast tomorrow.

Mum: It's okay, sweetheart. Just have a couple of bites and then I'll cook you some pasta and cheese.

Dad: We're not cooking extra meals every night. They need to eat what they're given. This is ridiculous. You know there are kids starving in Africa!

Kids: Send them this food then! We don't like it.

Sometimes there is war over digital media and games. Dad says the games are fine, but Mum says they're too violent. Curfews, homework, chores, eating, sleeping, friends, screens … the list of things we can disagree on is long.

The most common disagreement I hear about is this one:

'My partner and I can't agree on discipline. I keep getting accused of being too soft. I think that he is too harsh.' (Or vice versa … plenty of times Dad is the big softy.)

You'll note that I've made Dad the tough guy more often. This is not an accident. While there are countless extraordinary, concerned, involved, patient, compassionate dads – and dads bring tremendous strength to their family – the overwhelming majority of emails I receive are from mums who want help inspiring their male partners to rely more on love, emotion coaching and connection, and less on punishment and harsh words. Dads are still most often the disciplinarian. They see mums as being too soft. Mums are still most often the nurturers. They see dads as being too harsh.

(Perhaps this is the legacy of yesterday's parenting and the unfortunate reinforcement of strict and unhelpful gender roles: many of today's men were not allowed feelings or softness as boys, and that has society-wide repercussions now. Do we want to continue that gap between what men could be and what they're allowed to be into the future?)

Whatever the cause of this gender gap, too many parenting conversations go nowhere – or worse, in the wrong direction – because of the fundamental desire each partner has to change the other. It rarely works.

Creating change in others

Dr John Gottman is an internationally respected marriage and relationships researcher. He estimates that 70 per cent of what we don't like about our partner will never change. We can pester, cajole, threaten, complain, threaten some more or beg. Regardless, most parts of who they are just won't budge.

It is hard to shift habits. Expectations are challenging to adjust. And some things are part of our partner's nature. Plus, all that force that we exert creates resistance and resentment in our partner. If you've ever tried to convince your significant other they're not doing something right, my bet is that it didn't go well. Being told 'you're doing it wrong' is most likely to lead to an argument, hurt feelings and damaged relationships. Think about it for a moment: have you ever heard that phrase – 'You're doing it wrong' – and smiled at the person and said, 'You know what? You're right. Would you mind showing me how to do it correctly?' I didn't think so.

> **Mum:** If you keep doing it like that you'll only drive her away and make her afraid of you.
>
> **Dad:** Right. And so the namby-pamby soft approach is the right way, huh? You've got all the answers.
>
> **Mum:** All I know is that getting mad isn't getting us anywhere. It's not changing things. It just makes us feel horrible.
>
> **Dad:** Well nothing else has worked. I've had enough. I'm not playing this game any more. She needs to know I'm the parent and I expect more.
>
> **Mum:** It's not working.
>
> **Dad:** Fine. You do it. I'm obviously useless as a parent. I don't have a clue what I'm doing. You know what to do. So I'm out.

People don't like to be 'fixed'. The words, 'you aren't doing it the right way' don't often lead to positive conversations. This is especially the case when someone close to us is doing the fixing and correcting. Pride gets in the way. Each of us stakes out our territory and digs in defensively.

It makes sense though. While we all want to be better, most of us think the way we were raised is 'the *right* way'. I've met some people who are adamant that not only were they raised the right way, but it was 'the *one and only* right way'. The *best* way.

If we believe we were raised right, it's likely that we'll try to repeat what we know — even if that's a subconscious choice. And we'll likely react poorly when someone criticises our parenting. Not only are they criticising me. No … they're criticising my parents, too! They're saying my family got it wrong. And if my family got it wrong, what does that say about me? Am I deficient?

A dad once told me: 'I don't take advice about parenting from anyone except my parents and my wife.'

Statements like that prove two things. First, parenting is personal. And second, they prove that most of us who hold to such a belief are condemned to repeat the mistakes of previous generations.

More than that, though: these attitudes make parenting harder than it needs to be. Arguing with each other about the 'right way' to deal with a challenging child only adds pressure. Even though we don't like to admit it, most of us are making it up as we go along, trying to make it look like everything is under control and well thought out, but second-guessing everything we do. And, on the fly we all invent good reasons (or so we think) for the superiority of our approach. We defend our instincts at all costs.

When I talk with parents who are stuck, I hear them thinking, 'Wow. Parenting is one giant jigsaw puzzle: a 1000-piece puzzle, all ocean.'

Because of this complexity and our oft-times competing world-views, we struggle to get on the same page. And then we try to force changes in our partner. Ironically, Gottman has shown that when we accept our partner, they are more inclined to change their ways than when we are constantly at them to change. Our force creates resistance. Our acceptance leads to change. A caveat: they may not change the things we most want them to change … but then again, they might. Acceptance and enjoyment are the best fertilisers for growth.

When the expert and his wife don't see eye to eye

In the early days of my marriage to Kylie, I had no idea how to be a dad – or a husband. Kylie was educated in early childhood. And me? I was not educated in anything. My parenting showed it. But I would not listen to Kylie's advice.

As it became clear that I was ineffective, and potentially making things worse, I began my studies and changed my ways. Now we were on different pages again. Kylie didn't like taking my advice. After all, she had previously had the 'right' answers. Now I was making suggestions that were contrary to what Kylie had always thought was appropriate. While Kylie's answers *had been* better than mine, now it seemed mine might be better than hers, or so I thought. But Kylie disagreed.

Kylie began to resent me making suggestions based on what I had been learning. Until … I came into the house one day and things were loud and tense. Kylie demanded I take over because the kids were driving her insane and I *apparently* had 'all the answers'. So I did. And within about 20 seconds everyone was calm, the children were apologetic and peace was restored. (If only I did it that well *every* time.)

That incident allowed us to turn a corner. We're not entirely united in every aspect of our parenting, even now. I'm not sure perfect unity is possible. But we work together in consistent ways to get the best results for our children. And it makes such a difference.

So let's get on the same page. When we see things the same way – or at least work to understand one another – everyone gets along so much better. It's the first thing parents *need* to make their parenting work as well as it can.

Refusal

In some situations, your partner might refuse to discuss things with you. They may not even be willing to read what you're reading.

Please remember, you're playing a long game. So be the example as Kylie was to me, and then as I was later able to be for her. We both had many strained conversations about how to parent. (Even now we still do as our teenagers find new ways to test our skills.) In the end, patience was the winner. (There are pages and pages of practical advice and opportunities to work together in the final chapter of this book.)

In the meantime, *look for the good in the parenting of your partner*, or in step- and co-parents. While you know (and deep down, they know) that they can improve, so can all of us! But just because there's room for improvement, it doesn't mean they're an abject failure. Most parents, even those who struggle, are doing some things right. Enjoy those moments and express gratitude and appreciation when they occur.

It would be easy to focus on all the things that create division and misalignment. This probably won't be helpful at this stage of our discussion. Instead, let's focus on things that strengthen our views of one another.

What is one thing that your partner does with the children that you love?

How can you encourage him/her to do more of that?

What things do you enjoy doing together as a family?

1.

2.

3.

How can you create more time for those things?

Focusing on the things we love to do as a family will create far more alignment than focusing on our shortcomings, faults and weaknesses.

Where is our family going?

A farmer was spotted tearing along the side of the highway on a horse. He looked like he was in a big hurry. As he shot past one of the farmhands, the hired help yelled out, 'Where are you going, boss?'

The farmer yelled back, 'Ask the horse!'

Sometimes our partners and families are a bit like the horse. We're just hanging on while the horse races along out of control. So ... beyond same-page parenting around discipline, standards and expectations, we also want to get on the same page in terms of goals or vision. We need to have some idea where we want to steer our family.

Think about it like this:

We create plans for our businesses, for our careers, for our work lives. We develop financial and savings plans. We plan for our children's study or extracurricular pursuits. We plan our days. We make plans for all sorts of stuff. But no matter how often I ask whether people have a plan for their family, I'm almost always met with the same response ... Uh, nope.

Being on the same page means you're working towards the same vision/purpose for your family. And it will allow you to work on the small stuff – the details of how to make your family work.

Quick quiz		
Do you have a vision of what your family could be like?	Yes	No
Can you describe it quickly and easily to your partner?	Yes	No
Do you have a plan that is designed to lead you towards that vision?	Yes	No
Plan is set in stone?	Yes	No
Or are you making it up as you go along?	Yes	No
Do you think a flexible plan could be helpful?	Yes	No

Even in the small moments, it's worth recalibrating before you deal with a child and his challenges. You might ask one another these questions:

1. What do we value most in our family?

2. Are we okay with a child who challenges us or is perfect compliance our goal?

3. What is the most important thing our child needs to know from us?

4. If there is an unacceptable, intolerable behaviour occurring, how do we communicate that in a way that fits with our answers above?

5. What can we do right now – united – to move in that direction? (Or do we even need to do something right now?)

We're never going to be fully consistent with one another. Besides, consistency by itself is overrated. You can be consistently lousy. That won't help anyone.

Consistency is not helpful unless it's being consistent with the right things. So rather than trying to be perfectly consistent between the two of you, work towards being compatible and make sure you're compatible on the right stuff.

When we think 'they' are the problem

In my book *21 Days to a Happier Family*, I shared a story about Nicole, a mum battling with a daughter who had viciously cyber-bullied a student in her school. Nicole had berated her daughter and treated her like she was a problem. I stated: 'Nicole had assumed her daughter was the problem, and that was the problem.'

A parent shared the following experience with me about same-page parenting and Nicole's story.

> My husband has been speaking worse and worse about my
> 11-year-old son. He's been challenging us, but my husband's
> language towards him has been awful. My son never hears
> him, but my husband constantly mutters about how 'useless',
> 'painful', 'rotten' and 'awful' our son is. He keeps on pointing
> out all of the things our son does that are wrong and is giving
> him such a hard time.
>
> Whenever I tell my husband I don't like what he is saying
> and doing, he blames our son. Then I read Chapter 3 in *21 Days
> to a Happier Family*. I shared the story and stopped at the line
> that said seeing our child as the problem is the problem.
>
> My husband got really angry and defensive and told me that
> if our son wasn't the problem then I must have been saying
> that he (my husband) was. I tried to tell him I wasn't saying
> that but he wouldn't listen. I gave up and left.
>
> That night before dinner I heard unexpected laughter coming
> from the living room. When I walked in there, I saw my
> husband joking around with my son. They were goofing off and
> having fun together.
>
> In bed that night I asked what had changed. He told me
> that what I had said to him didn't make sense. It stung him

and made him angry. But when he had time to step away, he realised that there might have been something to the idea. So he tried to see our son as a struggling 11-year-old instead of a brat. It was like we were on the same page for the first time in ages, and it felt so good.

Not all stories work out so neatly. But the power of being on the same page is that our family feels harmonious, our children feel like life is predictable and, so long as the page is a good one, our children are more likely to thrive.

LONG-TERM INVESTING

Having a successful relationship with our partner or children is a lot like investing. The best investors in the world will tell you that to invest well, you've got to play a long game – put the money in every week and wait for 20 years until it matures. When the market is low you end up buying more because everything is cheap. When the market is high you buy less because it's expensive. But every week you invest. You just keep putting that money into that investment because you have trust and faith that, in time, you'll reap the rewards of the investment. The long-term compounding of your investment provides returns that are almost unobtainable any other way.

Our partner and our children experience our emotional investment in every interaction. When they're feeling lousy and down, we invest more. When they're feeling great, we still invest, but perhaps they don't need us quite so much, so we stay present and available and invest where it's needed. Then, after 20 years or so, we finally see the fruits of that investment. In most cases, wise investments compound day after day, year after year, and lead to remarkable returns.

But everyone has their own investment strategy. Some people prefer quick returns. Other people play the long game. Some investors are strategic and thoughtful. Others love to speculate and go for broke. Some are consistent, others less so.

Being on the same page matters as much in parenting as it does in investing, business, schooling or planting a garden. We need to get our investment strategy clear. That means we work together to identify what our goal is, the different pathways to get there and our preferred way. It also means preparing backup plans for when things don't go so well. We want to co-parent, regardless of our family circumstances, as intentionally and consistently as possible. Working as a team, we can fill in for one another and still be on the same page, acting compatibly because we've had the conversations and created an effective investment plan.

BIG CONFLICT

Sometimes conflict around parenting is so significant that the basic ideas in this chapter will not be enough. In these cases, there are a few things to consider:

1. **Get professional help.** Sometimes only one of you will be willing. This might be as much as you can do. If possible, however, work together.

   If professional help is not an option, a parenting 'mentor' might be less confrontational. Perhaps there is someone you and your partner see as an excellent parent. They may be open to a regular (weekly/ fortnightly) parenting conversation over a drink or an activity where you share experiences and ideas and trade suggestions. (We don't do vulnerability too well in our society – especially men – but a friendly ally rather than a distant professional might be helpful.)

2. **Experiment with different styles of parenting** for a few days to see how these approaches leave you feeling, and how they leave your children feeling. There are some risks with this, but if you pay close attention to what is in your hearts, and if you'll then be honest about how you feel, you'll find good answers.

3. **Agree not to fight about parenting in front of the kids.** Decide ahead of time that when decisions need to be made, you'll make them privately and in consultation with one another, rather than in front of the children. This ensures you don't undermine one another and promotes respectful conflict resolution.

HAVING THE LAST WORD

Every parent needs to remember that there is more than one way to raise a child. Just because you think *your* way is the right way or the best way doesn't mean that it is. We get deeply attached to what we think is right, often to the detriment of our family. So, being on the same page matters, but only to the extent that it provides stability, security, predictability and harmony. There is an argument that different parenting approaches can be beneficial. As long as the big stuff is agreed on, a differing approach shouldn't cause problems. And problems arise when parents don't support each other, but instead pull one another down – to the kids! Or when they shout over the top of one another to be right. Having parental disagreements can show children we all see the world differently and there's a way to live with that, as long as we do it with kindness.

Ultimately, we decide what matters most. We work out where we stand on it. We agree, disagree or find middle ground. (The Three Es of Effective Discipline in Chapter 4 will provide a powerful framework for parents to have these discussions.) Then, we get on with the job of raising wonderful children.

DECIDE

Now it's time to make a decision. Are you willing to get on the same page with at least some of these ideas? If yes, that's great. You're already on your way. If you can't be fully aligned at this point, work out what you can agree on, starting tonight. The focus should be understanding your partner's point of view and finding areas of agreement. Remember, if you say the diet starts on Monday, you're not really committed. Start now.

Take-home message

Raising children is a tough enough job already without opposition and antagonism from other adults who share in the responsibility. Researchers have noted that parenting on the same page increases family satisfaction and improves outcomes for children – so long as the habits of those parents are positive.

United parents don't do everything the same. You'll never agree on everything. But when there is a level of consistency between parents, and a willingness to work together to achieve the outcomes that we believe matter, we can create a sense of harmony and purpose in our family that is positive for our children and our partnerships.

2

Mattering and belonging

A little boy was itching to play with his dad. But Dad was too busy and kept putting him off.

'I'll play with you later mate.' Or, 'Listen buddy, I've just got to get this thing done and I'll be with you.'

One day Dad busily walked past the kitchen and saw his son taking some coins from Mum and counting them into his piggy bank. A few days later he walked past his son's bedroom and saw him counting coins on the bed.

As he sat at his computer one evening, emailing, his son walked over to him. Coins were jangling in his pockets.

'Dad?'

'Hang on a tick …' (typing furiously to finish the email.) 'Yes, mate?'

'How much do you get paid an hour?'

'That's a funny question. I get a lot. I think it works out at about 80 dollars an hour.'

The little boy's face fell. 'I only have 14 dollars.'

'What do you need money for?'

'I've been saving up so that I can buy an hour of your time. But I don't think I'll ever have enough.'

Now maybe I'm just a big sook, but that story gets me every time. Despite the predictable cheesiness, there is something about it that I resonate with.

Are you one of Mum's friends?

That story has a real-life version. One dad shared the following:

> I work in a job that involves international travel. I'm often
> gone at least three weeks each month, and sometimes more.
> But I quit my job and found other work (less well paid) when
> my four-year-old son asked, 'Who are you? Are you one
> of Mum's friends?'

We don't all have the capacity to quit our jobs, move to the country for that 'tree-change', or get hired help to allow us more time with family. Let's not be unrealistic. But our kids need us in their lives. The gift of time may be the most vital gift we can offer our children.

I consistently speak with people whose families are struggling. Fathers and mothers assure me, 'My family is the most important thing in my life.' Yet family doesn't factor in to their daily doings in any significant way. They're too busy. So let's also be honest about the amount of time we can devote to our family. If we really believe our family is the most important thing, why are work, fitness, study, book club, coffee, movie night, or some other priority, always being put ahead of family time? How do we have time to watch reality TV and play online games, but not to invest in our relationships? Yes, we need to get some 'me-time' to stay sane. But let's be real about how much time we *could* commit if we really meant that family time and the kids were the most important 'things' in our life. (You've heard the quote that *the most important things in our life aren't things*.)

Is 12 minutes enough?

A few years back, one of the larger law firms in the country hired me to run some parenting classes for staff. It was their parent network 'lunch 'n' learn' and 60 to 70 high-powered, thoughtful employees who were used to working 70+ hours each week were gathered to learn how they might better balance huge work hours with family commitments.

Prior to the event, I was briefed by an HR diversity manager. I was told that the lawyers worked on a six-minute billing cycle. Every six minutes (or part thereof) was one billable unit.

Then she asked one of the most bizarre questions I've ever been asked: 'How many billable units per day do parents need to spend with their kids?'

Me: Huh?

She explained that if I could give the lawyers a suggestion of how many billable units their children might need with them in order to be psychologically healthy, it would help them get the balance right. And it would reduce parent guilt for long hours worked and lack of availability.

> **Her:** What would be the minimally sufficient amount of time parents need to spend with their families to feel like they're getting the balance right? Would two billable units be enough? Twelve minutes a day? I found a study that says 12 minutes is enough. Will they be happy if you tell them that 12 minutes will do the job?

> **Me:** ???

This may be the most important thing I say in this chapter, so I'm putting it in italics for special emphasis:

You can't build a relationship watching the clock.

I can't imagine you've ever called out to one of your children and said, 'Okay. Time to talk. We've got six minutes. What would you like to talk about? Go! ... Wait. Time's up. I'll give you another six minutes tonight. Be ready. Don't waste it. I'm very busy and important, you know.'

This is obviously not real. But if you've tried to force meaningful conversation into a tight timeframe you'll know it doesn't work. It is almost impossible to be 'efficient' when building a relationship.

A woman sought my advice for connecting with her troubled and anxious daughter. I told her to sit with her patiently and listen.

> **Mum:** My daughter refuses to talk.
>
> **Me:** Sit with her, express your love to her, invite her to talk and then wait.
>
> **Mum:** Tried it. Doesn't work. She will sit there for an hour and not respond.
>
> **Me:** Be patient. Wait. Prove to her that you care more about her than the time on the clock.

A few weeks later I heard this:

> I sat with her and explained that I knew she was struggling.
> I hugged her. I told her I couldn't understand or help unless she
> shared things with me. She gave me nothing. After 30 minutes
> of me sitting and waiting, I asked again. Silence for another
> 20 minutes. Finally, after about an hour I said, 'Emmy, I'm here
> because you're my daughter and I love you. Tell me what's going
> on – please!' And she stared at me in anger and told me, 'You've
> ruined my life. Ever since we moved here my life has been the
> worst!' And finally the conversation started. We moved over
> a year ago and thought everything was fine, but she was still
> carrying that and wouldn't talk about it with us.

Time is the most important ingredient in our relationships. A lack of time undermines connection, puts pressure on every interaction and prevents the full expression of love. We know this. Yet it seems to be a crucial lesson that we, as parents, must learn and re-learn.

Most parents suggest these are the circumstances in which they get quality interaction and conversation with their children.

1. **In the car** – so go for longer drives than are necessary.

2. **Just before bed** – so let that bedtime experience take as long as it needs.

3. **During or after activities** – so get out and do things together.

There may also be a slight gender difference. Girls seem happy to converse face to face, while boys prefer to talk side by side. This may be purely due to conditioning. Or it may be built into our individual natures.

Think of the times you're most likely to want to talk with your partner.

Do you want to talk:		
The minute you walk in the door after a long day?	Yes	No
While you're watching your favourite show or scanning your social media feed?	Yes	No
While you drive?	Yes	No
In bed first thing in the morning or late in the evening?	Yes	No
At the dinner table?	Yes	No
While you're working together?	Yes	No
As you participate in an activity, such as a walk, ride or game?	Yes	No

When are your children most likely to be open to talking with you? Are there similarities? Most kids hate being asked about their day the moment they arrive home, or while they're doing something they see as important. But they tend to like chatting in the car, at the table or in bed.

Pay attention to the times your child is most responsive to conversation. Leave them alone at other times, and dive in to connect when it works.

It's important that we know when our children are most receptive to conversations. But how effective are we in those chats? Do we talk *at* them? Lecturing may feel good in the moment but tends to stifle two-way conversation, and it damages relationships.

Do we have an agenda? Feeling as though parents have manipulated things to 'set up' a conversation can reduce trust and disclosure. How well do we let the conversation breathe, and just listen?

STOP, LOOK AND LISTEN

Do you remember that ad from the TV years ago that taught us how to safely cross the road? It had a little jingle that I still remember, and sing to my children. 'Stop, look and listen, before you cross the road.'

The stop, look and listen instruction is a useful reminder to really take time to be there and listen to our children.

When we want to cross the road we stop, look and listen because there's a chance that something might be coming that could hit us. Small things like a skateboarder or cyclist. Medium-sized things like cars. And frighteningly large things like semi-trailers! Stopping, looking and listening helps us to safely navigate a physically hazardous or challenging situation.

In life, there is a constant stream of hazards – some very big and fast-moving – that could run over us or our children in a psychological or emotional way. If we aren't willing to stop, look and listen, we may miss something bearing down on us and we, our child, or even our whole family, could get hit by it. Perhaps it is a friendship challenge, an issue at school or a toddler feeling like she needs to be comforted. Maybe it's a child who wants us to acknowledge him as a person but doesn't know how to communicate that need.

To respond effectively to our children we *stop* what we are doing and pay attention. We *look* into their eyes as we speak with them and as they speak with us. We *listen* to what they say. But we extend our listening to ensure that we evaluate their body language, their facial expressions – even what their eyes are saying to us. This may not seem efficient, but ironically, it can often be a remarkably time-effective way to communicate and understand, because messages are sent and received clearly when we really pay attention.

When stopping for just one minute is not enough

We have all had that experience when stopping and listening to our child isn't enough. There are those times when one minute isn't enough. Our child might want to talk to us. For ages. About the most brain-numbing stuff in the world. And right when we are supposed to be doing other things that are 'really important'. Perhaps we asked how their day was and they decided to give us a second-by-second account of everything that happened. Maybe they're a really boring storyteller. Or it might be that they've experienced something that seemed traumatic that day: a teacher moving to a new school, being called a name in the playground, or receiving a poor grade on some schoolwork.

In those instances, we need to be careful. Sometimes it matters that we listen. Other times we might gently ask if we can talk about this soon. Make an appointment.

> 'Let's talk about this in the car in 20 minutes when we drive to your activity.'

> 'I want to hear what you are saying, but I can't pay attention right now because of what I'm doing. Will you set the oven timer for 15 minutes? I'll be finished this then and I can listen properly.'

> 'I'm on the phone but I really want to focus on you. Once I'm off this call can I come and get you?'

Make sure you make good on your promise. It helps your child know you think that they matter. And studies reinforce the power of this one thing. The children who grow up to be the most resilient, and have the greatest sense of who they are, are those whose parents showed they care by stopping and paying attention.

A rod for our backs?

Does thinking about this make you feel as though you will never get anything done? Will it just lead to more interruptions and selfish children?

Researchers have uncovered a surprising finding. Children whose parents are willing to stop, look and listen tend to become less needy. That is, they want *less* of our attention rather than *more*.

Reflect on your experiences as a child.

When you could not get your parents' attention did you:		
Sit peacefully at their feet and find a way to keep busy until they were ready?	Yes	No
Recognise that they had important things to do and use your initiative to find the answers on your own?	Yes	No
Find a sibling to tease or hurt?	Yes	No
Withdraw into your own world (or use a screen, book or toy as an escape)?	Yes	No
Pester them until they couldn't stand it any more and they lost their cool?	Yes	No

As an adult, when you can't have your partner's attention do you:		
Sigh gratefully because you didn't really want to talk to them anyway?	Yes	No
Do a funny dance because you know that getting their attention in this way will get you what you want?	Yes	No
Get frustrated, feeling unimportant and invalidated?	Yes	No
Walk out and refuse to talk?	Yes	No

Which of these would you most like for your child?

What is the best way that you can develop this outcome?

35

Researchers have found what parents already know from experience: failing to stop and pay attention to our children (or anyone who wants our attention) leaves them feeling lousy, and possibly believing that they are unimportant and do not matter. Beyond that, it often leads to bigger issues than those they were coming to us with in the first place!

When we stop, and listen, our children learn that when they need their parents, they'll be there. They feel secure in that relationship. Conversely, children who have parents who push them away, say 'not now' or tell them to 'hurry up' all the time, worry about whether their parents will be available – and they become needier, more clingy and more likely to demand their parents' focus at challenging times.

Soggy chips syndrome

I know hot chips are passé these days – we're all ordering our quinoa salads, right? But remember when you used to love calling in at the local takeaway for a carton of chips? The smell of the chips was (is) exhilarating. The cravings would (do) begin. We put our hand into the bag and lift out that piece of deep-fried potato in fresh oil. And we are immediately disappointed when we find out that the chips are a little cool and completely soggy. No one likes soggy chips. We like a hot, crispy shell surrounding a light, hot, fluffy centre. To bite into a well-cooked chip is a delight. Biting into a cold, soggy chip is only disappointing. But in that moment, we shrug, shove a few in our mouth and try to get the taste we were hoping for. Instead, the experience is often regrettably gross.

Our children experience soggy chips syndrome all the time. They try to get our attention. They want us to stop and pay attention for just one minute. That's the hot, crispy, fresh attention they want so much. When they can't get that kind of attention they become clingy, challenging, frustrating and resort to behaviour we can't ignore. Then, we respond with attention that is the equivalent of soggy chips. They don't get a hot, crispy shell with a light, fluffy centre. They get a cold, oily response that leaves them disappointed. But because they're so desperate for our attention, they'll take what they can get – after all, it's still attention, even when it's much poorer quality than they wanted.

When our child wants us, it can be easy to pretend to be listening while we continue to scroll through our social media or shoot for a high score on a video game. We might even turn our body and shoulders towards our child and mumble 'uh-huh' as they tell us about their day or whine about their sibling. And that leads them to act in ways that demand our attention … but it's not really the kind they want. It's soggy chips.

No doubt it has happened to you. You have talked with a spouse or partner, or a friend, and they've been distracted while you poured out your heart. It's frustrating! It erodes trust. It leaves us feeling like we don't matter. Our children feel the same way.

To build strong, trusting relationships with our children, the simplest things we can do are:

1. **STOP.** Stop what you are doing. Completely. Put down the phone. Turn away from the screen. Turn off the stove.
2. **LOOK.** Look at your child in the eyes. You might crouch down so you can hold hands. Make a visual connection.
3. **LISTEN.** Keep that mouth zipped. Just listen. Keep looking at your child and really pay attention.

Stop, look and listen makes people feel valued. (This works for spouses and partners, too.) They feel important. They know they matter. It creates resilience. It strengthens relationships. Try it today and watch how much better life feels.

A special note for dads

In all child outcomes, a father's willingness to stop and be responsive is central. Studies have shown that dads play a crucial role in guiding their children's development. And in many cases, they do things mums typically don't do. Data indicates that dads tend to add fun, colour and informality to family life. At the risk of being overly stereotypical, the same data pointed to mums tending to be the worriers, chastisers and punishers, while dads were more likely than mums to engage in vigorous play, such as rough housing and ball games, with their children. Dads have been shown to teach 'life skills' that mums often overlook. They get excited about physical prowess, competition and – believe it or not – fixing things! Now, I know this all sounds minor, but it gets important as the kids get older. The more Dad can be present and involved in his children's lives in a positive way (and sometimes just a safe presence is enough), the better the outcomes for them. Multiple studies, such as the one conducted by David Popenoe of Rutgers University, highlight that children growing up in fatherless homes are more likely to be involved (as adolescents) in crime, delinquency, premature sexuality, teen pregnancy, lowered educational outcomes, depression, alcohol and other drug use and abuse and, ultimately, poverty.

The reasons for dads being absent are many and varied. Some dads are distant through no fault of the family. They've chosen to step away. Other dads want, desperately, to be involved in their children's lives and cannot be present. Some dads work long hours and go away a lot. And if dads aren't safe, then of course they can only be present in ways that ensure the wellbeing of their kids.

Regardless of the reasons, the research is compelling and growing: dads need to spend time with their families. And when they are home, they need to stop, look and listen. When Dad is safe and caring, the more he is there for his children, the better the outcomes for everyone in the family.

What do you think your children would say if you asked them to respond to the following statements?

My parents stop and listen to me when I want to talk.	Yes	No
My parents console me when I am upset.	Yes	No
My parents show they care about me.	Yes	No
My parents make special times for me to talk with them.	Yes	No
My parents show genuine interest in me.	Yes	No
My parents remember things that are important to me.	Yes	No
My parents are available to talk at any time.	Yes	No
My parents make me feel like I matter to them.	Yes	No

If they are old enough, sit with your children and ask them how they'd respond to each of these statements. Engage in a conversation and really hear them. Take a close look at how much you agreed. If they said 'no' to anything, listen closely to find out why they feel that way.

As you talk with your children, ask them when you do these things well, and when you don't do things well. Ask them how you could do things better. Then make a plan together to be more available.

Be 'around'

If this all sounds like hard work, I get it. When they're young, children follow us everywhere. And sometimes that can be a pain. We want to shower in peace. We'd like our own beds back. Even the toilet – occupied – isn't off limits for our little ones. They want to be where we are. And talk to us. About everything.

It can feel mind-numbing.

The pressure eases a little bit once they get to about seven. Sometimes.

I have some good news for you. Children don't 'need' us to be forever in their faces, inquiring about their lives and making banal conversation.

A bunch of simple studies tell us that much of the time, our children just want to know we are close so that *if* they need us to stop for just a minute, we can. By simply being there, we act as a secure base and a safe haven. We're a retreat if things get scary. And we're a warm embrace when physical touch is needed.

Research with adolescents shows that even our teens like it when we're around, despite the way they act. There's that little thing deep down that makes them want to connect with us on some level. Connect, be close … but not necessarily talk.

It's not about spending 12 minutes co-building Lego every day. I mean, sure, if you were going to stare blankly at a screen, or if you're not taking any time to be with your kids at all, that might be a useful goal to set! But a better focus is to be there, to be close, to be available, as much of the time as possible. Unexpected conversations about both trivial and important things occur when we're available.

Our kids don't necessarily want to talk all the time, certainly not about all the important ideas close to their hearts, or the high-stakes relationships at school, or how they hope to change the world when they grow up. But just like us, they tend to like it when someone they love is respectful of their feelings and close by – perhaps for a hug, but often just to be near.

IDEAS FOR PARENTS OF TODDLERS AND PRESCHOOLERS

If your child is in day care or preschool, the following simple ideas can help you to stop for just one minute.

Connect

When you collect your child from day care, spend time right there and then to connect. Find out what they did. Talk about their activities. Let them show you around their experiences for the day. Be guided by them, though, and leave if they just want to go home. Keep the radio off in the car and chat, sing and make the commute count.

Devices down

The emails are pinging. The Facebook notifications are flashing. The texts are dinging. Ignore them. They may seem important, but they can (typically) wait until your child is in bed. Until then, keep devices down. The message we send to our children emotionally while we're messaging everyone else is clear: other people matter more than you do.

Invite them into your world

When you get home from work it will usually be hectic. There's dinner to prepare, a bath to run, a house to organise, preparations for the next day and, sometimes, even more work to do. When it's possible, invite your child into your world. Rather than sticking them in the corner with the iPad, get them prepping food or running the bath with you.

Touch

We easily forget how important touch is for a healthy relationship and a healthy child. Make sure you hug, tickle and touch. It builds bonds.

Ramp up routines

Predictability makes relationships feel safe, particularly for young children. If your little one knows that when you get home there is a set routine that is easy, fun and involves you both, they will usually be easy to work with, and your time together will be enjoyable. Set things up for smooth sailing by drawing up a chart you can follow together (but no stickers). It might include dinner prep, eating, bath, pyjamas, teeth, toilet, story, songs and bed. All of this routine increases security and safety, keeps your relationship together, reduces friction and promises you an easy night.

Night-time nurture

When it's bedtime, tuck your child in, then start a conversation about the day. Talk about sunshine (grateful things), storm clouds (challenges) and rainbows (overcoming difficulties) from their day. Ask what they're looking forward to the next day. Tell your child you love her. Make bedtime super special.

Traditions

Make the most of the time you have together by establishing some simple and fun traditions. It might be a daily tradition of back-scratches before bed or a fun wake-up song each morning. It could be a weekly tradition like watching a movie and eating a pizza on a Friday night or having a Super Saturday treat each weekend. You could have a monthly tradition like a camping trip or journey to the same special place. Traditions build memories, strengthen relationships, establish a sense of identity (this is who we are) and make life fun.

Respond actively and responsively

There's a psychological phenomenon called 'mattering'. That's what this chapter, and the next, are really about. Do your children know that they matter to you? Mattering is crucial for building feelings of worth and value, and growing resilience.

The table below shows four ways we can respond to our children when they talk to us. Some of them highlight to our children that they matter. Others don't.

	Destructive	Constructive
Active	Cynicism	Delight/Interest
Passive	Dismissal	Acknowledgement

Let's start at the bottom. Let's say your child has just won a race.

Passive and Destructive comments are dismissive and ignoring. We're saying things like, 'Yeah, whatever.' Perhaps we are a little kinder, with a glib, 'Oh, okay. If you say so.' We may even add, 'I need you to put your things away please. If you leave them out here someone will tread on them.' I know what you're thinking … that feels horrible. That's because it is. Unfortunately, it happens.

Next is Passive and Constructive. This is a low-energy, delayed response where we acknowledge what's gone on and stop right there. Our child runs to us and says, 'I won my race!' We say, 'That's good news.' We don't actively build the conversation.

An Active but Destructive statement might be, 'Did you see who you were racing against? It was a bunch of kids who have never done a day of training in their lives. Wait until you get some real competition before you go getting a big head.' This is clearly an active, elaborative response, but it is tearing down, rather than building up.

The response that is best is Active and Constructive. We find out our child wins the race and we say, 'I saw. It looked like you gave it everything! How do you feel?' As our child tells us more, we encourage positive and engaging conversation.

It doesn't sound so hard, does it? We do it naturally with babies. But then they get bigger and we get bored or distracted ... or annoyed. And from time to time we need to be prepared to hear some mind-numbing story that devolves into numerous tangents before finally getting you to a confused state where you'll offer ice-cream or lollies just for a moment's peace!

But think about how good it feels when someone responds to *you* actively and constructively. That is, they engage you with eye contact and interest. Then they work with you to constructively build the conversation. This says: 'I care about you. You matter. I want to connect with you.'

To respond actively and constructively we need to just stop for one minute, look our children in the eyes and listen. Then we show interest and build the conversation. It is one of the most important things parents can do for their children.

Dollars drive our economy. Fuel drives our cars. Attention drives our relationships.

Take-home message

When your children need you, stop and really pay attention. Don't simply turn your body towards them while still keeping your head facing the screen. Don't humour them by saying, 'Uh-huh, yep, I hear you,' if you're not really listening.

Stop what you are doing. Look them in the eyes to show you are paying attention. Listen. Respond in an active, engaged way. Then pay attention to the results you get compared to normal.

Our children need us to be available, to nurture them. In practical terms this means that they need us to just stop for one minute. Or 12. Or however long they need.

Being understood

'Oh. You're getting quite emotional. This is wonderful. We can learn vital life lessons together now.'

It's not a statement many parents say out loud. Like when you cut their sandwiches into rectangles but they wanted triangles.

> **Parent:** Oh! Big emotions. Excellent. Let's listen to one another and learn from this.

Or they come to you for the fourth time to dob on their sibling for teasing.

> **Parent:** Yes! Now we can really be close and spend some time connecting over your discomfort with your sibling.

Or they can't find their sports uniform or their *other* shoe.

> **Parent:** Ah. I can see that we'll all feel better if we sit together and experience these emotions productively.

It can be even harder when you tuck your children in at night and say, 'I'll see you in the morning,' and then you walk out of the room praying you are right ... but then you see them five times before 5 am (at which point, they're ready to start the day and you're ready to collapse!).

One dad told me he had this conversation with his four-year-old son:

Dad: Mate, you've been getting up too early. I don't want you getting out of bed until at least 6 am

Son: Okay, Dad.

Son: *(comes into bedroom at 2 am)* Dad, is it six o'clock yet?

When I heard this story, my heart melted. I saw a little boy who wanted to please his dad and be obedient. His dad only saw a son who was annoying and creating maximum inconvenience at 2 am! When we choose not to understand, we choose an egocentric view. We only see things from our point of view.

Imagine if Dad was open to understanding.

Dad: I wasn't expecting to see you, son.

Son: Uh-huh.

Dad: Would you like to tell me why you're here?

Son: I need a hug.

Dad: You got it. Come here. *(Hugs)*

Dad: Anything else?

Son: Is the sun awake yet?

Dad: No, it's not six o'clock yet. Let's go back to bed and when the sun wakes up and you can see without the lights, then it's time to get up.

Or perhaps Dad could set an alarm for his son and let him know that when it goes off he can come in and say hi.

An understanding, compassionate approach to our children's feelings, fears, anxieties and experiences leaves them feeling safe, and leaves us feeling peaceful and caring.

She never listens

Parents fail to understand what their children are going through far more than we'd like to admit. Many years ago, a father described his difficulties with a teen daughter. Her constant disrespect eventually got too much and he lashed out at her in anger. She was physically hurt and left home. He and his wife contacted me for help.

I asked a question of him:

> **Me:** Why is she challenging you?

> **Him:** The reasons are irrelevant. Regardless of how she feels, she needs to show respect, and if she can't show it, she shouldn't expect it. She never listens to a word I say!

He was angry. Ironically, he wanted her to listen to him but he was unwilling to listen to her. He was demanding respect in a most disrespectful way.

We discussed things you'll read about in this chapter: recognising that she is learning and doing the best she can, understanding developmental processes, empathising with her emotional state, trying to access and appreciate what was occurring in her life that she was unwilling (or unable) to disclose and being patient with her humanness before setting appropriate limits together. But the man was resolute.

I have reflected on this incident countless times since. While this book is about younger children, the principle remains the same. Sometimes our children will give us experiences we don't really want to have. They refuse to pick up their toys. They won't eat their food. They keep bringing home their uneaten lunch from school. They leave wet towels on the floor. They fight with siblings. It's a long list. As part of each of these challenges, there is a significant emotion that our children will show us, and it's usually inconvenient and unwanted.

When our child becomes emotional, what kind of a parent or leader are we going to be? Are we going to be the kind of parent who flings their garbage back at them in disgust? Will we be doormats, humbly thanking them for it and cleaning up after them? Or is there another alternative?

From time to time I have imagined this young teen girl's dad responding with understanding. I suspect that it might have gone something like this:

> **Daughter:** Just get off my case, Dad! You expect perfection. You're always telling me what to do. You've got no idea!
>
> **Dad:** *(calmly and softly – even though he's bursting with frustration inside)* It feels like we're always on your case lately, doesn't it? And it's driving you mad. I can hear how frustrating it is for you.
>
> **Daughter:** You just don't stop! You're constantly telling me what to do and that what I do isn't good enough. Ever! I'm 15, Dad! I'm not a little kid any more.
>
> **Dad:** *(with kindness)* Yeah. I hear you. We probably need to spend some time understanding how it is for you a little more. Would you be open to talking with us?

I have imagined that instead of experiencing escalating feelings and violence, this girl would have felt safe and understood. And Dad's response is not far-fetched. We can all respond like that. You see, our emotions are like a jacket. We choose which ones we'll put on and take off. As parents, our job is to not only wear the right emotion, but to help our children with theirs, whether they are age 2 or 22.

Grateful for empathy

Before I returned to school to pursue my undergraduate and PhD studies in psychology, I was a young 20-something radio announcer. At a specific point in my career I was underperforming badly. Kylie and I had just had our first baby – a little girl – who was very sick for several months. She was not sleeping, which meant we weren't either. And we were exhausted. My performance at work was slipping. And eventually the inevitable occurred. I was called into the boss' office so he could give me some much-needed feedback. I sat at the table and waited for him to start flinging my poor work back at me in disgust. He clearly wasn't going to be a doormat.

After a moment, he commented that '… things seem a little tough right now'. His understanding broke the ice, but I was still on guard. I agreed I wasn't doing too well, but offered little in the way of excuses. Then he surprised me. 'What do you need? It seems like you could do with a little help at this point in your life.'

The man who had the power to sack me, or at least warn me of all the ways my performance was jeopardising my career and demand I pick up my game, simply offered to help me – in the same way a parent might offer to help a child who is making a mess of things.

Had my boss done what many parents or leaders might ordinarily do, I would have left the office dejected and potentially even passive aggressive. Instead, I walked out of his office grateful, inspired and motivated to be better. He had put himself in my shoes, imagined how life felt for me and then asked how he could help. What a gift!

We want to be understood. It's essential for us as adults. We often find it difficult to provide the same vital understanding for our children.

———————————————

How often do you find yourself doing the following to your children when they challenge you, experience big emotions or act in ways that are not in keeping with your expectations?

Give advice:

What you need to do is …	Always	Sometimes	Never
If you would just be kind, this wouldn't have happened.	Always	Sometimes	Never
If you'd have listened to me the first time …	Always	Sometimes	Never
If you would stop being such a baby, that situation would have turned out differently.	Always	Sometimes	Never

Talk about your feelings and experience instead of theirs:

I understand. I totally know how you're feeling. I get it.	Always	Sometimes	Never
I remember that happened to me once.	Always	Sometimes	Never
You don't know how lucky you are. When I was a kid …	Always	Sometimes	Never
I know just how you feel.	Always	Sometimes	Never

Make the child's pain seem unimportant:

Seriously. Cut it out. You're driving me nuts.	Always	Sometimes	Never
Would you just grow up?	Always	Sometimes	Never
Everybody suffers. Get used to it. You're not that special.	Always	Sometimes	Never

When children feel bad, they feel their pain is so bad that no one can really understand it. That's why a person who is hurting would probably rather have you say, 'Your pain must be awful. I wish I could understand just how sad (or hurt or lonely) you feel.' Sometimes the best way to show understanding is to admit you can't understand just how bad a person feels and instead offer, 'That seems so hard and upsetting for you.'

Seeing the world through a child's eyes

It's counter-intuitive. When your child is acting out, welcome the opportunity that creates. We want to do the opposite. But that doesn't work so well. When the dads I wrote about earlier got mad about 2 am wake-ups and teenage disrespect, their relationships were not nurtured and their children did not feel understood. Behaviour deteriorated. If my boss had been angry about my poor behaviour rather than seeing how I was struggling, I would have wanted to quit.

From time to time our children seem to be intent on causing chaos, destruction or violence. They delight in nastiness. Regardless of the behaviour and what we perceive the intent to be, children act in challenging ways because they feel out of control, unloved or incapable.

Form follows *feelings*. That is: our children behave the way they feel. If they feel lousy, their behaviour is lousy. If they feel great, safe, loved and understood, they behave positively – even perfectly. We tend to not be so great at seeing things the way our children see them, though. We see things from our adult perspective, in which children are so … childish! They act foolishly and cause us immense inconvenience.

We've forgotten what it's like to be a child. We've forgotten the anxieties and nervousness, and even the fear of getting things wrong or disappointing our parents. We've forgotten what it's like to not understand.

We can try to take our child's perspective, but we consistently find it hard to see through their eyes.

This is something that our children themselves may not be able to do yet. Developmental researchers have identified an important capability called 'Theory of Mind'. Studies suggest that from around age five we develop the capacity to see the world through another's eyes – of taking their perspective. Prior to that, the brain is too immature and undeveloped to recognise others might have an alternative perspective to their own. They are entirely egocentric. It's all about them. They don't care if we disagree. It's irrelevant. Their view is the *only* one.

(If you are not sure whether your child can take another person's perspective, have them show something to their Nanna over the phone – without FaceTime or Skype – just talking into the phone old school. Young children will say to Nanna, 'Look!' and they'll expect that because *they* can see what it is that they are pointing at, so too will Nanna. Of course, this is impossible because Nanna is somewhere else! But little ones don't get that. They think, 'If I can see this from my perspective, so can Nanna.' Once their perspective capability kicks in – that is, once they've developed Theory of Mind – our children understand that just because they can see things one way, it doesn't mean others can also experience the same perspective – especially if they're in another place.)

But just because adults can see another perspective, it doesn't mean we do. In fact, people with power (like parents) are less empathetic – less likely to look through another's eyes – than those with less power. We become impatient and demanding. We seek compliance. We get absorbed in solving our problems rather than understanding theirs. As one brief example, social psychology professor Paul Piff, from the University of California Berkeley, conducted a study that showed drivers of luxury cars were less likely to stop at crosswalks or intersections when compared with drivers of less luxurious cars. There's less willingness to see the world through another's eyes when status and power exist in the relationship.

Stop being a wuss and jump!

I recall a powerful experience in perspective-taking that highlighted just how poorly I was taking my children's perspectives and understanding their feelings. Our family visited an indoor rock-climbing centre. Typically, when you climb, you need someone below you attached to your rope to 'belay' you. If you fall and they're on belay, they can hold the rope and stop you falling.

At this centre, some 'auto-belay' machines had been installed. To use one, you simply connected the rope and carabineer to your harness and began climbing. The rope would automatically retract into the roof.

My eight-year-old was climbing on auto-belay, reached the top of the wall and realised she would not be able to descend unless she jumped. She had to let go of the wall and hope that the auto-belay would catch her. She was too scared. Being at least ten metres up in the air, it was a long way down. She didn't want to let go of the wall and trust that this rope hanging from the ceiling would automatically catch her.

I had to spend considerable time talking to her, encouraging her to trust me and to trust in the system. 'It will catch you, Annie.' I was empathic. I was understanding. But I was also thinking it wasn't such a big deal. I could feel my impatience increasing. I wasn't scared. There was nothing scary about it. Why wouldn't she just jump?

Eventually my calm voice and persuasion got us a result. After several minutes, she finally let go of the wall, pushed away, felt the rope adjust to her weight and was lowered gently and safely to the ground.

It all seemed over the top and too hard. So much emotion over such a simple thing.

About ten minutes later I had scaled a wall. It was my first time using the auto-belay and when I reached the top of the wall I hesitated. It was time to let go … but I was nervous. What if the machine failed? What if it wouldn't hold me? What if it caught me too late?

I climbed halfway down the wall until I reached a point where I was stuck. I couldn't descend any further. I climbed back up, then descended again hoping for a different outcome. No joy.

An employee walked underneath me. 'Hey!' I called out in a whisper. 'If I let go, will this really catch me?'

He looked at me, chuckled and then offered reassurance. Summoning all my courage, I finally let go of the wall and fell to the floor, breaking my ankle. Not really. I'm just kidding. But that was my great fear. What if? Instead, the machine caught me and lowered me softly and gently until I was on the ground.

As I unbuckled the carabineer it occurred to me that I had been lacking in empathy for my daughter while she was on the wall. I intellectualised her anxiety. I *knew the words to say* to show I could *see* how she felt. But until I had my experience on the wall personally, I had no idea how it felt to have those feelings.

A safe haven

Right at the start of the chapter I made the point that we rarely feel a thrill of excitement when a child is experiencing a challenging emotion. Yet that is precisely what our children need from us. The late Dr Stephen R Covey said, 'the greatest human need is to be understood'.

How well do we really understand what is in our children's hearts, experiences and lives? Do we really, *deeply*, know what they worry about, are afraid of and are comforted by?

Is it even realistic to think we might have to be understanding all the time? Isn't that a bit over the top? Wouldn't it be too much like cotton-woolling our children?

We get so involved with the demands in our lives that we don't notice and don't respond to the invitations to be a part of our children's lives.

Dr John Gottman calls these invitations – whether civil or uncivil – bids for connection.

And the best times for talking and connecting? Whenever your child makes a bid to connect.

———————————————

How to *really* listen so your child shares more.

1. **Begin with the end in mind**. When your child wants (or needs) to talk, decide at the start what you want them to remember. Do you want them to remember your kindness and compassion? Do you want them to remember your listening ear? Unconditional love is shown by giving complete and unconditional focus.

2. **Minimise distractions**. Stop, look and listen. **Stop** doing anything else. Put screens away. Be still. **Look** into her eyes. Your child won't be able to focus on you if you are a moving target. **Listen** to what they want to say. When they invite you into their lives, they want *all* of you.

3. **Be open to connection**. You might say, 'I really want to hear what's on your mind. Tell me what you're thinking.' This ensures you send a signal that you're ready to listen.

4. **Have soft eyes**. An elderly grandmother told me this was her favourite parenting advice. When she softened her eyes towards her children she noticed her voice softened, her posture opened, her words became more compassionate and she stopped hurrying. Soften your tone, your posture, your words and your timetable by seeing them through loving eyes.

5. **Channel your ideal parent**. Think about the best parent you know and listen the way they would to their child – or to you. Think about how precious this child is (normally) to you. This will help your child feel like their thoughts, experiences and opinions matter. You might call this 'fake it till you make it'. You could even just imagine that ideal parent was watching you. We tend to parent best when we have an audience.

6. **Aim to build**. Regardless of whether your child has done something wrong, find something right and positive. Express appreciation.

7. **Be flexible**. Sometimes there's noise or other interruptions at home. Be willing to go for a walk (and take the dog for the exercise and companionship), grab some wedges and sour cream from the café, or do something together (plant something, water the garden, wash the car). Doing encourages talking.

Challenging emotions and behaviours can ruin relationships or become opportunities to connect and strengthen family ties and increase feelings of safety.

When we act as a safe haven, our children will be calmer and kinder faster. They'll feel secure. And they'll be open to us offering our understanding with statements like, 'Tell me more,' or 'You seem frustrated about things.'

It's crucial to dive into a problem-solving discussion when emotions are at lower levels. If we try to connect when emotion has built up (or is high), we often miss our chance. Our child is not ready to hear us while their emotions are elevated (or off the charts). We need our child to be calm so we can communicate. When emotions are high, no one listens particularly well (remember: form follows feelings). This means we need to work with our child so everyone calms down.

There is a trick here: we often assume that telling children to calm down will help get calm. Have you tried that?

You: Would you calm down? *(Rarely, if ever said in a calm way.)*

Child: *(Screams more)*

You: I said calm down! Calm down, calm down, calm down!

Child: Oh. If you put it like that, I can be calm.

Said no child ever. 'Calm down' doesn't calm us, and it doesn't calm our child. The opposite is true. 'Calm down' makes them feel pressured and pushed.

How do you respond when another adult tells you to calm down in *your* poorer moments? Do you take that advice on board and settle in for a conversation? Rarely! The typical response is, 'Don't *you* tell me to calm down!' Instead of calm, we get its opposite: agitation and anger.

'Calm down' is crucial, however, because trying to be logical with someone who is emotional rarely works. Big emotions often bring a narrow range of options (and some would say they also bring irrationality!). So rather than trying to jerk our child back to a calmer temperament with demands like 'calm down', we *need* to join them in their distress, upset or pain and walk by their side towards peacefulness. In some instances, they may prefer space and alone time. In other cases, they may prefer some 'time in' with us, being close.

An old counselling technique is to remind people that their feelings are like a train going through a tunnel. If we interrupt the feelings too soon, it's like trying to smash through the walls of the tunnel. It doesn't work. The mountain is on top of us (or our children). But when we stay in the tunnel and ride the emotion all the way to the end, it eventually subsides. We find ourselves in peaceful daylight again. We think clearly and rationally. We become resilient. Our job, as parents, is to sit with our children during those big emotions and help where we can. Then in those times where helping doesn't help, we simply ride through the tunnel with our children. They come out the other end and we have conversations with them that would have been impossible in the middle of the tunnel. They feel heard, understood, supported and validated. And they come up with resilient and positive solutions *when they stay in the tunnel until the end.*

It's not about behaviour

Most parenting programs (but certainly not all) and popular approaches to parenting (like the Super Nanny) are built less on an understanding approach, and more on a behavioural approach to behaviour. When a child behaves in a way that the parent doesn't like, they seek to change the child's behaviour through punishments (time out) and rewards (praise).

But if we can accept and respond appropriately to our children's emotions, they feel understood and their behaviour changes accordingly. They absolutely *need* limits. I'm not suggesting that we let them do what they want and that we coddle their precious emotions. But rather than trying to control, manipulate or force our child, we are taking an inside-out approach. We are helping them to be calm enough to find answers within themselves and work with us to do what's right. And the evidence shows it can be profoundly effective. Children with identical IQs at age four are well ahead by the age of eight when they are emotion-coached by sensitive parents.

Rather than dismiss or disapprove of our child's strong emotions, we need to understand them. Our kids need us to be emotion coaches. Emotion-coaching parents see their children's challenging moments as an opportunity for connection. They engage, share enough information to begin the conversation and then back off. They just ask, 'What can you tell me?' Then they wait. No criticism. Just opportunities to talk.

I asked Marc Brackett and his team at the Yale Center for Emotional Intelligence to share their steps for helping parents work with their children and understand their emotions. His colleagues Robin Stern and Kathryn Lee shared the following invaluable information about their evidence-based approach to emotional intelligence: **RULER**.

RULER is an acronym for the skills of **R**ecognising, **U**nderstanding, **L**abelling, **E**xpressing and **R**egulating emotions. Being skilful in emotional intelligence means being smart about your emotions – recognising and understanding them – and using them to meet your goals.

We know that our kids are watching us and learning from us. We want to be great role models. RULER helps us to be emotionally intelligent by sharing the way we are feeling (recognising our emotions), being curious about what they are feeling (recognising their emotions), sharing what we understand about what caused our feeling and asking our kids what caused their feelings (understanding emotions), using and encouraging a nuanced vocabulary to communicate the specific feeling we have (like the difference between disappointment and frustration), expressing our feelings and encouraging our kids to express theirs in the right way, at the right time and to the right degree. And most importantly, regulating – and co-regulating – our kids' emotions. That is, effectively managing emotions.

Here are some tips that can help you practise RULER skills to help kids feel understood and families to build stronger relationships and greater wellbeing overall.

1. **Pay attention**. We all have feelings all the time – they come, they go – they're all okay. Emotions are signals we can learn from; they carry important information and can help us connect with each other.

2. **Feel your feelings**. Our feelings make us human. Noticing and naming our feelings helps us know ourselves better and make smarter decisions. We can all be better at enhancing feelings that make us feel better, and calming the ones that don't.

3. **Talk about your feelings**. Engaging in conversations with family members about feelings helps everyone learn, feel safe and manage feelings well.

4. **Listen**. Listen to understand – not to judge, deny or dismiss one another's emotions.

5. **Be curious**. Being curious 'emotion scientists' about ourselves and others can lead to discoveries that enliven our relationships and help us understand our thoughts, feelings and behaviours. Getting at the underlying feeling and its cause is critical to providing the best support.

6. **Show empathy**. We all want to feel understood. While we may not agree with one another's actions, it is important that we try to accept and understand one

another's feelings. When we do this, we build emotional safety, trust and closeness.

7. **Choose your response wisely**. Having feelings is different from acting on our feelings. We don't have to react immediately to something that someone says or does, or be derailed. We can slow down (breathe), feel our feelings, think about our best self and choose a response that we feel proud of, rather than regret.

8. **Remember there's more than one view**. We often feel we're right, but there might be another way to look at any situation, without necessarily making our view wrong. Sharing different points of view within a family can be healthy.

9. **Stay connected**. Take time every day to reach out to loved ones to let them know you are thinking about them.

10. **Have the courage to repair**. After an argument or being disappointed in a loved one, don't be afraid to be the first to reach out. Say you're sorry if you know you've hurt someone's feelings.

11. **Add a dose of kindness**. Your relationships will be warmer, and when you look back on your life, you'll be glad you were kind and compassionate to one another.

When our children become emotional, we have the potential for magical moments for connection. We need to be able to understand so we can help. Haim Ginott said, 'Statements of understanding should always come before statements of instruction.' We need to respond to emotions first, then invite children into a conversation about solutions and limits.

Other things to understand

Since understanding is such a vital human need, we should briefly take a look at other things that need understanding when it comes to our kids.

Understand they're doing the best they can

Sometimes our children do things that appear entirely stupid and irrational. (So do adults. You may have been accused of this at one point or another.) It can be tempting to call them stupid and irrational! If you've read this far, you know that I'm going to suggest a better approach.

When others do things that make no sense to us we need to remember that those things typically make perfect sense *to the person doing them*! We just don't understand their *why*. Our children are almost (but not quite) always doing the best they can. And even when they're fighting or ignoring us, it makes sense to them.

If we can engage in understanding (as opposed to lecturing), we'll usually find that things can be sorted out quickly and painlessly. Often we'll see a clear logic in their behaviour. It may have lacked skill or foresight, but it will make sense.

Understand they're human

The more I've considered my own parenting, and the longer I've watched other parents, the more I've come to recognise something that makes me uncomfortable. We want our children to be perfect. We seem to have little tolerance for mistakes and we dive in quickly and consistently to correct errors of judgement and behaviour. It's almost like when we had children we expected that things would remain convenient and easy, that we'd be able to control them the way we'd controlled our careers, our home-making, our travel plans and creative endeavours. And all too often we get our children in trouble less because they've done something wrong, and more because they've inconvenienced us or made us feel we weren't in control of a situation.

They may be tired and behave poorly. They need understanding. (Note: don't tell them they're tired. This rarely leads to good outcomes.)

They may be forgetful. They need understanding. (We can be forgetful too sometimes.) Does this mean we take their jumper to school so they don't freeze, or their lunch so they don't starve? That depends. The better we understand the context, the easier it can be to determine the best way forwards.

They may be lacking a skill. For example, perhaps they bully someone because they want to be friends. Understanding that they're human means we adopt a different stance and are less likely to dismiss or disapprove.

I said it earlier, but it bears repeating: our children aren't robots (and nor are we). We're all human. We get it wrong. We can be inconvenient ... yes, even us! Our ability to tolerate our children's less convenient and controllable, more challenging moments well, and guide them effectively, will pay dividends as they grow up feeling understood and knowing how to show empathy to others because of our modelling.

Understand context

When we step back and see the big picture, we may be less inclined to dismiss or disapprove of our children's emotions. Frustratingly, unless we patiently turn *towards* our children, we often have very little access to their challenges and no appreciation of their struggles.

Perhaps a child is playing up at home. We can get mad (disapprove and turn against). We can ignore (dismiss and turn away). Or we can understand (turn towards). Perhaps we'll discover that our child's friend has moved away – or just moved desks!

One dad told me his eight-year-old was being 'a big sook'. She was disruptive, hurting a sibling and ignoring Dad's best efforts to 'make her calm down'. He stopped, paid attention and focused on her. He acknowledged that this wasn't normal for her. And he spent quiet time with her (about 90 seconds) to show he cared.

> **Dad:** *(calmly, kindly, gently and compassionately)* You're having a horrible day and you're mad at everyone.
>
> **Daughter:** *(snuggles in to Dad, sniffles and nods)*
>
> **Dad:** I'd love to help you. Can you tell me a bit about why you're struggling?
>
> **Daughter:** *(nods and slowly opens up, crying the whole time)* I just woke up feeling tired this morning and my legs hurt and then my brother said something nasty to me and I feel awful.
>
> **Dad:** Oh. It's hard when mornings don't work out the way we want them to, and when people treat us in ways that feel rude.
>
> **Daughter:** I know. And now I feel mad and I want to be left alone.

In this situation, Dad had no access to his daughter's earlier experience with her brother, or the growing pains in her legs. He had no appreciation of how hard her morning had been because, like any of us when we're not employing empathy, he was only aware of what he could observe. Lots of important information is missing. Ironically, he told me he had wanted to threaten her and tell her to go to her room if she was going to be nasty to her siblings! Clearly, this would have been unhelpful for their relationship, and ignored the underlying reasons for her challenging behaviour.

Children don't play up for fun. Behind *all* challenging behaviour is an unmet need. Understanding the context more deeply helped this dad understand and work out useful ways to guide his little girl more effectively.

Understanding milestones

At the time of writing, my youngest is three. You've probably noticed that children around that age don't like wearing clothes. I still find myself sneaking up on the munchkin, clothing in my hands, hoping to catch her and get them on her, even if it's just for the ten minutes we'll be at the shops.

It would be easy to be frustrated. But understanding her development means it's easier to laugh about it, let it go where I can, and only make a big deal about it in those instances where clothing is no longer optional. Of course, if she were several years older it would be developmentally inappropriate for her to run around the house in the nuddy, but at this age it's no big deal.

It's the same with the dad whose son keeps waking up at 2 am. Frustrating, but developmentally appropriate.

I've got something for you, Dad

When one of my children was one year old, I heard her talking in her cot one morning. Realising she was awake and needed me to help her, I walked into her room. She smiled in excitement. Any parent knows the feeling – you literally feel like the most important person in the world when they look at you and smile like that (because you are).

I walked towards her and as I did so, she held out her hand, clearly wanting me to take what was in it.

Worried that it might be something sharp or poisonous – 'hypervigilant parenting' – I held out my hand and said, 'Ta to Daddy.' (I should clarify that we don't allow our children to sleep with sharp, poisonous things … but kids seem to find stuff they shouldn't have everywhere!)

My little girl smiled so proudly at me as she placed a nugget of poo in my hand – it was as though she felt she'd given me the most priceless gift ever.

I looked at my precious, helpless little baby and commented, 'Wow, thanks for letting me know you need my help when you did. I'm glad I got here right away.'

Can you imagine how gross it might have got if I had been just a couple of minutes later?

This is obviously disgusting! And inconvenient. But it's typical for a new toddler who is learning to explore the world. Getting mad at her is not honouring her developmental progress.

As our children age, the frustrations could continue unless we understand where they are on their developmental trajectory. A six-year-old boy cries and gets in trouble from his dad because '… boys don't cry. You need to stop carrying on like a sissy.' But our children don't learn to regulate their emotions particularly well until around age eight – and we all know adults who still have challenges with their emotions, all too often because those emotions were dismissed or disapproved of when they were children. (Not to mention how toxically sexist that kind of instruction is! Boys *do* cry and they must be allowed to feel soft, vulnerable feelings as much as their sisters. If we continue to perpetuate boys' discomfort and disengagement from their feelings, we will only perpetuate the toxic masculine culture that affects our sons *and* daughters.)

Our teens resist instructions, argue and ignore boundaries. I don't know any parents who aren't upset by this, but it's developmentally appropriate. They're pushing for independence. (As mentioned earlier, it doesn't mean we completely accept all behaviour. We need to establish boundaries together. But this is best done when emotions are positive and people are feeling safe. We'll discuss setting limits in the next chapter.)

Children typically follow a general and predictable pattern of growth and development. They naturally mature and learn the things they need to learn at specific times. Our job is to provide a safe and nurturing environment, rich with opportunities to learn and grow. Often we become impatient because development is too slow. For example, we might be irritated by the 'terrible twos'. We want compliance. They want to push boundaries and do what feels good! When we understand that this stage is a vital one for learning to be more independent, we can be more patient and even grateful for our children developing when and how they are! None of us want our adult children to act like infants. But we shouldn't be surprised when our infants act like infants. That's appropriate. Each stage of development is important as children move towards adulthood.

Differences in development

A quick note: some children develop faster or slower than their peers. A child may seem particularly mature – or immature – depending on his developmental processes and environment. This is normal, too. Kids slow down and catch up all the time. Often some characteristics are well developed. We may think of a child as gifted, yet they possess underdeveloped characteristics in non-academic areas. And when times are stressful, conflict-ridden or tense, it's not unusual to see a child temporarily regress to less mature behaviour. It's also critical to note that the milestones we take for granted are based on children growing up in predominantly white, wealthy, Western nations. Children in other circumstances may experience milestones entirely different from our kids' milestones. Understanding development means we set expectations appropriately and experience more peaceful parenting as a result.

Take-home message

When we turn towards our children with understanding, we are not focusing on their behaviour, but instead we are focused on their feelings. If our children were icebergs, their behaviour would be what we see above the water, but the larger part of the iceberg rests below the surface. This remains invisible unless we take the time to understand what is down there. Feelings, developmental progress, the broader context and more, each contribute to our children's behaviour. As we understand those things, we can help our children manage their behaviour rather than us having to be the ones doing all the managing, all the time. A focus on feelings brings better short- and long-term results in our children's behaviour, maturity and development.

Something better than punishment

A farmer was out the front of his farmhouse doing chores one morning when a big four-wheel drive pulled up in the driveway. A man in a uniform climbed out of the vehicle, walked up to the farmer and stated, 'I'm here to inspect your farm for any illegally grown drugs.'

The farmer responded, 'Fine. But I'd recommend that whatever you do, do not go into that paddock over there.' He pointed behind the man to a beautiful paddock.

The officer replied, 'Mate, I don't think you understand. I'm here to inspect your farm and I have the authority of the state government – the premier – behind me.' He reached into his pocket and pulled out a badge. 'Do you see this badge? It means I can go onto any land I want! Have I made myself clear?'

The farmer apologised and resumed his chores. The man walked away to begin his inspections. A short while later the farmer heard a scream. He looked in the direction of the paddock he had pointed out as the one the officer should not enter. Sure enough, the officer was the one who had made the noise. He was racing across the paddock as fast as he could, a raging bull in hot pursuit – and gaining fast.

Seeing the imminent danger the officer was in, the farmer stepped onto the fence that surrounded the paddock and called in a loud voice to the officer, 'Your badge! Show him your badge!'

As parents, we do a lot of badge-showing. We sometimes think that just because we are the parents, we can do or say whatever we want and our children should follow our instructions. But often, our children are a little like that bull. They don't want to be told what to do, and showing them our badge – our authority – makes zero difference.

We say things like, 'Because I'm the parent. That's why.' We make demands that they do this or don't do that (like going into the paddock). They don't seem too concerned about our requests. So we get mad. We start throwing our power around.

H.L. Mencken said, 'There's always a well-known solution to every human problem – neat, plausible and wrong.' I love this quote because it highlights how our simplistic strategies for 'fixing' our children can create greater challenges than they solve. Children *do* need to know that we have power. We should use our power to demonstrate that they are secure. They need to know we'll use our knowledge and capacity to keep them safe in situations they don't have the ability to handle. But using our power to coerce, compel and control will rarely lead to effective learning and limit-setting.

When they don't listen, we get mad, yell, threaten, remove privileges, ground, and some parents even use physical force and hit their children. But *doing things to* our children by punishing (or scaring) them *ignores the reasons* for their challenging behaviour. It ruptures our relationships with them. And, paradoxically, it reduces the likelihood that they'll listen to us when we try to teach them. It makes things worse, often in the short term and almost certainly in the long term.

It seems that the more we rely on our authority (our parenting 'badge') to 'make' our children do things, the less authority we really have. Sure, we have it while the children are under surveillance, but once we turn our back, our authority is gone.

It works the other way, too. I recently had a run in with my two youngest daughters. As I walked away, I heard myself mumbling at them, 'You're not the boss of me.'

Power struggles

Power struggles are an inevitable part of parenting, and they start early on. For toddlers, it's wanting to stay up late, sleep in Mummy's bed, eat ice-cream for breakfast, have Daddy feed them – no: Mummy … no: Daddy – or wear zero clothing. Actually for toddlers, everything is a power struggle.

For bigger children, maybe it's wanting more screen time or to keep playing instead of tidying up. Or wanting that treat after you said no. For teenagers? How about even more screen time, extended curfews, wanting to drive a car before they're ready or drink alcohol before they're ready (or both).

Our children need us to set limits. I believe that they actually *want* us to set limits, even though they fight them like crazy. When we limit certain behaviours, our children know that we care about them. Implicitly, they understand that we set limits precisely because we want them to be safe, happy and healthy. Children without limits tend to have poorer outcomes throughout their lives than children with limits, but it's a delicate balancing act because children who have strict limits also often have poor outcomes. It almost sounds as though you're damned if you do and you're damned if you don't.

The truth is that the number of limits our children have is far less important than *how* those limits are set. When we set limits in lousy ways, we get lousy outcomes, regardless of whether there are a few or a lot. When we set limits in positive ways, we get positive outcomes, and again the number of limits is irrelevant.

How are we doing discipline?

Australian parents (and parents around the Western world) typically rely on punishments to discipline their children. These include smacking, time out, withdrawal of privileges and grounding. Parents also commonly threaten, yell and bribe.

In previous books, blogs and interviews, I have spent significant time outlining evidence against *all* of these 'discipline' strategies. A recent study that reviewed over 50 years of research confirms that smacking, for instance, brings *no benefits* whatsoever. In fact, both short- and long-term impacts of corporal punishment on children are negative in every variable that is measured. It seems clear that smacking does for your relationship with your child what hitting your partner might do for your marriage.

Data on other forms of discipline is not so clear, but consistently points to a rupturing of relationships between parent and child and short-term compliance when parents or an authority figure is around. Compliance drops off once the surveillance stops.

In short, kids learn to hate their parents when their parents hurt them, ignore the reasons (and emotions) underlying their difficult behaviours and turn their backs on them when they need help.

Despite the science and the logic, many parents still argue that smacking, threatening and hurting children through punishment is appropriate and useful. Alternatively, parents will reason that non-violent consequences (a euphemism for punishments), such as time out or withdrawal of privileges, should be used to 'teach kids a lesson'. Too many parents believe that hurting and punishing children will make them better, wiser, more patient, considerate and compassionate. It does not. Instead, it damages them.

When SOMETHING has to be done

There are times when we need to remove a child from a situation, or remove an object from a child, so they don't break things or hurt others. There may also be times when we remove privileges as a direct 'consequence' (yes ... punishment) of their behaviour. But these situations will ideally be kept to an absolute minimum. (They also occur less frequently than many parents think.) They'll be dealt with based on the principles throughout this chapter and book. If we cannot get compliance or reason, we may need to take action. But we want to do it as kindly and calmly as we can. Then, when the child is ready, we want to talk it through and focus on teaching, not hurting. When punishment (via smacking, yelling, hurting, removing privileges, grounding, time out, etc) is our go-to, we can get results but they're usually short term and ineffective.

Even if a parent thinks these punitive reactions to children's errors of behaviour are appropriate, many will agree that it's *never* the best thing to do if we want to help our children thrive. In a caring relationship, there is no room for punishment. Only teaching and loving, caring guidance.

What's the point?

This prompts the question: *what is the objective of discipline?*

There are some who say that discipline exists to make our children sorry for their 'bad' behaviour. But punishing a child tends to make them sorry for one thing only – that they got caught. One mum told me her kids tell her when they've done something wrong because they want the attention! This is a classic case of soggy-chips syndrome.

Mum: He's just doing it for attention.

Me: So, give him attention! And then, when things are calm, explain expectations and create a plan to improve his behaviour next time he wants attention.

Others argue that punishment is to exact a price: to obtain retribution. I've spoken to many parents who are certain that when a child does something 'wrong' (I prefer the term 'challenging'), that they should be hurt. A price must be paid. While it is true that we should teach our children to make things right, or repay what was taken, or make restitution in whatever way is appropriate, our focus, again, should be on teaching and guiding. Not hurting.

Making children sorry, or making them pay, hides the true purpose of discipline. Discipline should be designed, not to make our kids afraid of doing 'that' again, nor to make them sorry (although done right, they will feel sorry). Rather, discipline should be designed to make our children *better people.*

It's the motive that matters

Marshall Rosenberg stated:

> Two questions help us see why we are unlikely to get what we want by using punishment … The first is: *What do I want this person to do that's different from what he or she is currently doing?* If we ask only this first question, punishment may seem effective because the threat or exercise of punitive force may well influence the person's behaviour. However, with the second question, it becomes evident that punishment isn't likely to work: *What do I want this person's reasons to be for doing what I'm asking?*

The trust triangle

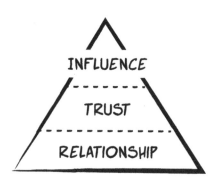

The primary purpose of discipline is to influence our children, ideally in ways that align with strong and compassionate values and principles. Our influence will typically come in one of two ways:

1. power; or

2. a relationship of trust.

The police represent a useful illustration of power. When you drive down the street and see a radar or speed camera in operation, it is influential. You slow down (even if you weren't speeding). Power provides short-term influence and compliance. But in the same way that it does little to make us safer drivers except in the immediate circumstances, power does little to make our children better – except when we are there with our badge, to demand and coerce.

If our children are being forced to do something, they're not being responsible. They're being compliant. Force creates resistance. And force requires surveillance.

Building a relationship of trust is the slow, long game. It is the investment that pays off over time.

Fast is slow, slow is fast

We build a relationship of trust by meeting our children's need to know they matter and that they are understood. As they feel safe around us, knowing they can rely on us, they trust us. Then we can teach and guide in ways that help them become better. Slowly.

We want to help our children be better people *all the time*, rather than only when we are watching them. Getting our relationship right builds trust, which leads to powerful influence.

Kids aren't co-operating? A common parental response is to blow up or threaten, shout and carry on. We might ridicule, dismiss, demean or ignore. Or we bribe, dangle carrots and go for the sugar-coated quick-fix. In each instance, we rely on our parental power. This is the fast approach.

But fast is slow. We have to keep doing it again and again. We don't get a consistent, lasting result.

Let's do a quick parenting assessment.

Do we:			
Use threats as punishment with little justification?	Always	Sometimes	Never
Give in to our child when he/she causes a commotion about something?	Always	Sometimes	Never
Yell or shout when our child misbehaves?	Always	Sometimes	Never
Find it difficult to discipline our child?	Always	Sometimes	Never
Punish by taking privileges away from our child?	Always	Sometimes	Never
Scold and criticise when our child's behaviour doesn't meet our expectations?	Always	Sometimes	Never
Use physical punishment as a way of disciplining our child?	Always	Sometimes	Never

Threaten our child with punishment more often than actually giving it?	Always	Sometimes	Never
Punish by putting our child off somewhere alone with little if any explanations (time out)?	Always	Sometimes	Never
Grab our child when being disobedient?	Always	Sometimes	Never
Explode in anger towards our child?	Always	Sometimes	Never
Scold and criticise to make our child improve?	Always	Sometimes	Never
Smack when our child is disobedient?	Always	Sometimes	Never
Threaten punishments to our child but don't follow through?	Always	Sometimes	Never

These approaches are the 'fast' approaches that end up taking more time because of the way they damage the foundations of our trust triangle. They either do too much, or in some cases, too little. The more you have ticked 'always' or 'sometimes', the more likely it is that influence will be undermined by overuse of power.

The following pages will emphasise how to shift from a 'fast', power-based approach to a 'slow', relationships-based approach.

That's because our kids don't learn to do the right thing for the right reasons. They only learn to do the right thing when we are around so that they can get the goody or avoid the punishment. So their moral development is slow. Their progress into responsible, thoughtful, considerate, autonomously motivated individuals is slowed or even stopped when we go for 'fast'.

Same goes for doing things for the kids when they can't do it themselves. Fast means we just do it. We'll teach them later!

And slow is fast.

Slow requires considerable effort in the early phases. It's about laying a solid foundation in the relationship – one of trust, compassion and emotional availability – and spending time in effortful dialogue, guidance and teaching.

This stuff is slow, and it can be hard work.

But as time goes on, it is required less and less. And soon enough, slow becomes fast. Children trust us, learn from us, come to us for guidance and love to be with us.

When our children are doing the wrong thing we spend time with them. We speak quietly. We listen. We are patient. We consider their preference to wait until the ads, or until they lose a life in their game. When we *have* to hurry, we talk with them clearly but kindly and explain rather than demand.

It is this slow approach that helps us get our relationships with our children right. This leads to trust being built, and ultimately, it creates remarkable influence. This process, built on slow, patient listening and understanding, is the heart of effective discipline.

The Three Es of Effective Discipline

I used to teach a number of discipline strategies, but now I primarily focus on one: the Three Es of Effective Discipline – Explain, Explore and Empower.

These three Es are not steps, but are a fluid process. Sometimes we Explain and move to Explore before reaching Empower. Other times we Explore, then Explain and then Empower. Often, we will dance between them, starting where the circumstances demand, revisiting them multiple times during the course of our discipline conversation.

Explain

Sometimes it feels like 90 per cent of parenting is repeating the same sentences over and over again.

Are they deaf? To test this with my children, I stood at the door and whispered ever so softly, 'Who wants ice-cream?' It took a moment to register ... and then they came running. All of them.

When we ask our child to act a certain way, do they know why? Or do we simply make demands and, if our children dare to ask why, respond with, 'Because I said so, that's why!'

Under normal circumstances, the best approach is to stay calm and kind, and then Explain what you're after and why. We get the best results when we provide a reason for what we're asking.

> **Parent:** When you leave your wet towel on the floor, it gets mildewy. The carpet stinks and the towel gets ruined.

> **Parent:** When you don't replace the empty toilet roll, it means someone else ends up in a potentially embarrassing situation.

> **Parent:** When you leave your lunchbox in your bag, it smells bad. Plus, we get stressed out the next morning when we can't find it. Same with your shoes. When you leave them in the car and on the front deck and in the garage and at your friends' house, we get stressed the next day when we can't find them.

Parent: Fighting with your brother makes everyone angry. I'd like you to find a way to play nicely, or play separately.

Partner: Sweetheart, when you leave your socks on the floor I end up having to pick them up. I'm already looking after three children and it makes me feel like I'm your servant rather than your equal.

You may be thinking that I'm teaching you how to suck eggs. Fair enough. The idea of explaining does seem kind of simple and obvious. But it's worth considering how often we really explain things to our children and how often we *think* we've explained them. Moreover, as the issues become more complicated, carefully reasoned explanations become important. That's something parents of teens deal with all the time.

Increasingly, parents of kids between 8 and 12 are now needing to begin some discussions around issues we typically think of as necessary for teenagers only, including screen use and social media, alcohol and other drugs, pornography and so on. When we discuss these complicated topics, 'because I said so' simply will not work. Start explaining clearly with the little things and it is easier when we get to the big things.

Explain also may be viewed a different way, however, and this is where it becomes a powerful disciplinary tool.

What happens when someone starts explaining things to you? There may be times where you listen intently, making mental notes, nodding and working hard to absorb their information. But, sometimes, you probably find yourself nodding off and wondering when they'll stop. You've probably seen your child's eyes glaze over as you begin your well-rehearsed speech about why this or that needs to change.

A better approach is to invite your child to explain the reasons why – to you.

Parent: I saw your wet towel on the carpet in your room. Can you tell me why it's important that we hang our towels up?

Parent: We had a toilet incident today when that guest of ours didn't have any paper. Can you tell me why that could be a problem?

Parent: We seem to be having a lot of lunchbox challenges lately. What have I asked that we do about lunchboxes each day? Why do you think I've asked that?

Clearly, these are again simplistic, but they illustrate the point. When our mouth is moving, our child's mind isn't. When their mouth is moving, it requires their brain to function! A more challenging situation may be:

Parent: You have asked me, several times, if you can have Instagram. I'm reluctant to say yes because you're eight. I know your friends have it. But why might I prefer that you don't?

Annie looks after the office at the Alannah and Madeline Foundation. (This Annie is not my daughter – aged just ten at time of writing. This is another Annie.) Some time ago Annie changed the sign on one of the doors. It used to say, *Please Shut the Door.* The new sign says, *Please keep this door closed as it helps to regulate the air conditioning.*

I asked Annie, 'Why did you change the sign on the door?'

Annie: No one shut the door.

Me: Well, how's compliance now?

Annie: It's amazing. Almost everyone closes the door.

Me: Why do you think that is?

Annie: I think it's because now they know why we want it closed.

Let's do a quick parenting assessment.

Do we:			
Emphasise the reasons for rules?	Always	Sometimes	Never
Explain to our child how we feel about the child's good and bad behaviour?	Always	Sometimes	Never
Give our child reasons why rules should be obeyed?	Always	Sometimes	Never
Explain the consequences of the child's behaviour?	Always	Sometimes	Never
Help our child to understand the impact of his/her behaviour by encouraging our child to talk about the consequences of his/her own actions?	Always	Sometimes	Never

These are some of the simple ways that we can Explain. The more you (and your children) identify with an 'always' response, the more effectively you are explaining.

Rumi said, 'Raise your words, not your voice. It is rain that grows flowers, not thunder.'

This is our first bite at the top of the trust triangle. We're going for influence by providing (or asking for) clear limits and guidance regarding what we expect. Sometimes Explain works well enough that no further discipline is required. But in real life it usually isn't enough. It may even be counter-productive to spend too much time here unless the issue is simple. That's when we move to (or start with) Explore.

Explore

In the previous chapter, I made the point that our children's behaviour makes perfect sense to *them* even if we cannot understand it at all. If all we ever do is explain, then we'll never understand the reasons for those things they're doing that seem so wrong. We need to Explore. Seeing the world through their eyes is essential for effective discipline. How can we teach and guide when we don't understand?

Explore means that we stop talking and we listen. We encourage our children to open up and tell us how they see things.

This part of our discipline process is centred on the bottom two levels of the trust triangle. Think of those attributes that ensure we get our relationship right with someone so that there is trust between us. Explore is about that part of the process.

This is more than going through the motions of 'You tell me how it is for you ... and then I'll tell you how it's going to be.' Instead, this is the process of accessing that previously unknown information and perspective from our child.

> **Parent:** You seem to be really struggling to deal with the mess on your floordrobe. What is making things so difficult today?
>
> **Parent:** Having an Instagram account is a really big deal to you, huh? Can you tell me why this matters so much to you?
>
> **Parent:** Can you tell me why you don't feel like being kind to anyone in our family today?

Another way to show patience is to calmly ask, 'Are you still thinking about what I said, or do I need to say it again because you missed it?' Such questions can be useful with children as young as two or three. They are helpful because our children can sense that we care. They experience our empathy as we seek to understand how things are for them.

Exploring should be done with genuine care. We can't really feel what our child feels unless they are willing to let us into their private world. They'll only do that if they trust us. And they'll only trust us if they are experiencing a relationship with you based on caring, listening, understanding, showing respect, having integrity, humility and honesty.

Ironically, once they open up and share, they seem to be acknowledging to themselves that they can trust us, and they become open to our influence. At this point, it seems logical that we tell them precisely what we expect, and what they must do. However, we actually get better results when we do the opposite and listen to understand more.

Let's do a quick parenting assessment.

Do we:			
Get close to our children when they experience sadness?	Always	Sometimes	Never
Treat sad and angry moments as natural occurrences?	Always	Sometimes	Never
Encourage our children to talk about their troubles?	Always	Sometimes	Never
Lend an ear when family members feel unhappy, fearful or angry?	Always	Sometimes	Never
Give comfort and understanding when our children are worried, angry or sad?	Always	Sometimes	Never
View our children's anger as instructive and useful?	Always	Sometimes	Never
Focus on understanding why our children are feeling the way they do?	Always	Sometimes	Never
Feel confident that our children will not develop bad character traits just because they're feeling sad, angry or worried?	Always	Sometimes	Never
Respond to our children's feelings with patience and understanding?	Always	Sometimes	Never
See our children's fears and worries as normal and valid?	Always	Sometimes	Never
Explore our children's angry feelings?	Always	Sometimes	Never
Use times of unhappiness, fear or anger to show each other support, offer guidance and help each other solve problems?	Always	Sometimes	Never

The more you (and your children) identify with an 'always' response, the more effectively you are exploring.

Empower

Now that we have our children's trust and they are open to our influence, we gently Empower them to find solutions within themselves. We say something like, 'Thank you for helping me understand how you're feeling.' Then we add:

'What do you think we should do about it from here?'

'Where to now?'

'How can we solve the problem?'

If our children are a little older we might ask, 'If you were in my position, what would you do about things?' This allows our child the opportunity to see things from an alternative perspective. It can be powerful for them to step away from their own view and put themselves in another's shoes. Mature responses are common, if you allow them this latitude and encourage empathy. (Another alternative is, 'If you were making the rule for your little brother/sister, what would you think they should be allowed to do?')

When they share 'dumb' ideas, ask for more ideas or for explanations. Problem-solve. If they get stuck, tell them to go and have a think and come back to you when they're ready. We want our children to come up with the way forwards. They do so much better when we get them engaged in the process.

Remember, ultimately you do not need to solve the 'problem' – they do. And if they can agree to go and play without upsetting one another, that's the end game.

Does this mean we don't have limits? No way! It means that we work with our children on how to move forwards rather than doing things to our children because we're mad and we want to 'teach them a lesson'.

If they've broken or ruined something, they need to recognise that it ought to be fixed. We guide them there by asking great questions. 'How are we going to fix this? Who should be responsible? How will you pay for it?' (We don't demand that a three-year-old pay for it, but they can be involved in cleaning up the mess once emotions are calm enough.)

If they've hurt someone, they need to apologise. But forcing it is pointless, so we guide them. 'What do you think is the best way to make things better? How do you want our family to work?' (More on this in the next chapter.)

Let's do another quick assessment.

Do we:			
Give our children input into rules, solutions, strategies and routines?	Always	Sometimes	Never
Show respect by encouraging our children to express their opinions?	Always	Sometimes	Never
Feel comfortable with our children having a difference of opinion with us?	Always	Sometimes	Never
Consider our children's preferences when making plans that involve them?	Always	Sometimes	Never

'Always' responses indicate a willingness to empower our children to make decisions autonomously, or interdependently.

When nothing else works

Sometimes you'll Explain. You'll Explore. You'll Empower – and you'll get nowhere. Life with children is messy and tough from time to time. What do you do then?

It depends.

Sometimes they're tired. Or hungry. Or too angry to reason with you. If that's the case, let the issue die down. Feed them. Give them sleep or space.

When things are calm you'll have better conversations, a happier family and less need for punishments (or consequences).

What if the problem keeps happening?

There are still some situations where children struggle to improve. You'll explain things again and again. You'll be understanding and empathetic and try to see things through their eyes. You'll leave it up to them. No result. Backchat, laziness and issues remain.

If your child is being oppositional, then consider the following three possible explanations:

First, think about your timing. If you keep asking your children to do things at times that do not work for them then you'll get resistance. They may be in the middle of playing. (This *is* important, despite you feeling it's trivial.) They could be tired. There may be any number of other reasons your timing is impacting on their willingness to respond.

This means you're dealing with an issue around control and autonomy. No one likes being told what to do all the time. And let's be real for a minute. Most of our interactions with our children consist of us telling them what to do, when to do it and how to do it. We are constantly correcting and directing.

Do they need to do stuff? Absolutely. But it can help when we allow some flexibility (where possible) around timing or even the tasks that need to be completed. Parents need to balance empathy with wisdom. Sometimes we're flexible because we know it matters. Other times we're firm because, well, we know it matters. Each situation is unique. Regardless, when movement is required, conflict often occurs no matter how empathic we are. Transitions can be tough and sometimes there's little we can do about it.

Second, consider your tone. Are you speaking kindly? Or in a way that would make anyone want to get away from you? If we're getting frustrated it shows in our voice. So speak softly, make eye contact and be simple, clear and direct.

Third, is what you are asking reasonable? Sometimes we ask more of our children than they can manage. Perhaps they need to tidy their room but it's so messy they're overwhelmed. Maybe you asked them to feed the dog or run some rubbish to the bin but it's dark outside and they're scared.

This means there may be some kind of competence or mastery issue. While it's true that we shouldn't be doing things for our children that they can competently do for themselves, there are times when this rule needs to be broken. It might mean spoon-feeding your five-year-old because he's too tired to do it himself. It could mean helping your 11-year-old to tidy her room because it's such a mess she doesn't know where to start. A compassionate approach gets more done and preserves our relationship.

If you're still getting no joy, surely consequences and punishments are okay? Here's what I do in my home.

> **Me:** Children, get off the screens now. It's time to get ready for bed.
>
> **Children:** Dad, we just need a few more minutes.
>
> **Me:** I gave you your ten-minute warning 12 minutes ago. And I gave you a five-minute warning as well. Would you like to turn off the screen, or would you like me to do it?

And then I stand there and count (in my head) to ten. If I don't get a response:

> **Me:** Did you not hear me or are you still thinking about it?
>
> **Children:** *(keep staring at screen)*
>
> **Me:** Okay. Time's up.

I turn off the screens. They whinge and moan. I stand firm. They go to bed. I hold onto the devices until the next day.

Do we need to punish our children? Do they need consequences?

Sometimes they need to be removed from where they are for the safety and wellbeing of others. Sometimes that might feel like a punishment. But if we Explain why we're doing it, and then once things have calmed down, if we Explore what's going on for them, and then we Empower them to make better decisions in the future, we'll typically find they'll do better than if we hurt them or disempower them by removing privileges to 'teach them a lesson'.

When our children feel safe from anger and punishment – even when they get things wrong – they can trust that we are there for them. Our children will be more likely to learn from their errors and poor decisions when they feel they can come to us and talk with us ... be empowered by us. They need to know it's okay to make mistakes so long as they learn to be better in future.

The 'consequences' of behaving in challenging ways should not typically hurt. They should, instead, revolve around teaching and learning to be better next time. And that is entirely up to us.

The saying 'fight fire with fire' is the antithesis of effective discipline. When we get upset with our child who is 'upset', we are in *our* world rather than theirs. We make demands that they conform to our expectations. They don't feel that they matter. They don't feel understood. Ultimately, the 'fire' comes from both ends – from us and from our children – and it burns out everything in its path. But water (love, kindness, compassion) puts out the fire and leaves something to work on.

If you're really struggling with this, try the following exercise.

Next time your child requires 'discipline', imagine that she or he is not your child. Instead, s/he's one of the neighbour's children, and you're looking after her/him. Chances are, you'd deal with someone else's child by explaining, exploring and empowering. This means you'll work with them, rather than doing something to them to force compliance.

Does age matter?

Because young children (under about four and a half or five) don't understand another's perspective, this process can feel futile. Age matters somewhat here.

For children under the age of two, I recommend nothing but love and cuddles. Correction can wait. Even from the age of two until three (or ideally four), we want to re-direct, distract and gently teach by giving clear explanations or asking for them to explain things to us. In these first years of life, the softer and kinder we can be as we teach and guide, the better. Even when your daughter flushes her socks, undies and various other clothing items down the toilet because you've taught her that dirty stuff goes there, we want to focus on gentle teaching, not punishment. (You don't know fear until you hear that flush followed by a cheerful 'bye bye'.)

The Three Es of Effective Discipline work for children (and adults) from around age three onwards. We need to tailor our language and instruction to be appropriate for different ages, but the principles are useful across all age groups.

My friend Peter Cook is a devoted dad who cares deeply about parenting. During a discussion he shared a simpler version of the three Es for younger children. It goes like this:

Draw two circles side by side, overlapping slightly. In one circle, write the words *Parents' Decisions*. In the other circle, write the words *Children's Decisions*. Explain to your child that there are some decisions that parents make for their children regardless of what they think. And there are also some decisions that children get to make with no input from parents.

Ask your child to identify some examples of decisions that parents make. Then ask your child to identify decisions that you stay out of.

Next, draw an arrow from the overlapping component of the circles.

Write *We Decide Together*. Now explain that some decisions are made by negotiation.

Once you've made it clear that you are the parent and you are responsible for certain decisions, power struggles will shift. When there's a bit of pushback you can smile and say, 'This is a decision that is in the parent circle.' That's the end of the story. Sometimes your child will sulk. There will still be occasional screaming and arguing. But the line has been drawn, the expectation is set and many power struggles will be defused. So long as we don't abuse the power we have as parents, our children can feel secure with us calling the shots we need to call and either negotiating with – or deferring to – our children for other decisions.

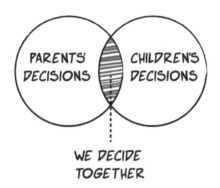

One more important point: as your child matures and develops, your circles will change size and change in the extent to which they overlap. Negotiations will become increasingly common. This is healthy and normal. We start to focus far more on Exploring and Empowering. It also suggests that this idea will work for older children as well.

At some point a major shift will occur. The circles will almost entirely separate. And your circle will shrink while theirs enlarges. You will push increasingly large amounts of responsibility onto your child, making yourself redundant. And you will have raised an adult.

Discipline works best while they're young

A guru was walking with his pupil through a forest. He paused in front of a waist-high sapling and asked the pupil to pull the sapling out of the ground. The pupil grabbed it with both hands, gave a big yank and the sapling broke free from the soil.

The guru nodded approvingly and the two walked on briefly before the guru stopped again, this time in front of a tree that was head high. Again, the pupil was asked to pull the small tree from the ground. After ten or 15 minutes of grunting and groaning, sweating, leaning, leveraging and digging with sticks and rocks, the tree finally came loose.

Turning around, the guru pointed to a tree that was a metre thick and 20 metres tall. 'Now this one.'

The pupil just laughed. 'Not possible without some serious machinery.'

'Yes, that is right,' responded the guru. 'This is how habits work. The older they get, the bigger they get. Their roots go deeper. And they become more and more challenging to remove or retrain.'

The sooner we start to teach our children well, and the earlier we encourage empathy and perspective, the more likely it is that they will grow to be both strong and caring people.

Take-home message

We need to be caring allies in our children's development. But all too often, we become punishers and enforcers. By taking an approach that ensures we build a strong relationship that promotes trust, we create the opportunity for influence. We do that best by Explaining, Exploring and Empowering.

5

Getting along with others – including siblings!

Kylie and I felt like we were coping just fine with two kids, but once we had our third daughter and we were outnumbered, we buckled under the weight. Wow! Talk about hard core. I'd wrangle one, Kylie would grab another … but who was going to look after number three? And once they started pulling one another's hair, biting, scratching or throwing things at each other, we realised we were in for some challenges.

A friend with four grown children commented, 'It's just the first 18 years that are the hardest.'

But rather than incriminate my children for their sibling squabbles, I'm going to dob in a couple of mates. Ben and Jay were two of my best friends growing up. They are brothers, only about 18 months apart, and they introduced me to the concept of sibling rivalry. Their family lived on the side of a ridiculously steep hill in North Gosford. The backyard was all lawn, but it was on an angle that would wear out an Everest Sherpa!

We used to play cricket on a level strip in their yard about three metres wide that ran from one end of the yard to the other. The house was at the top. The slope ran about one quarter of the way down the hill to the flat strip, and then continued to the bottom of the yard. The ball only needed to travel 150 centimetres down leg side to be a certain four runs.

Once it was off the level strip and rolling down that slope, there was no stopping it before it made it to the fence.

In every game we played, sportsmanship became the central issue.

Jay: Dad, Ben's being a bad sport!

Ben: No, I'm not, Dad! It's Jay. He's doing bad sportsmanship!

Jay: I am not. Dad, Ben's lying. He's being a bad sport!

Ben and Jay fought about everything. They were close in age, super competitive and regularly needed to be separated as conflict erupted into very unsportsmanlike conduct. I would stand and stare while the boys bickered and, from time to time, brawled. They were great mates. They just hated losing to one another.

It's not just the competition between siblings for our attention, or more time on a device before 'it's my turn', that drives parents crazy. It's the conflict. Sibling rivalry, competition and squabbles are seemingly inescapable. They cause tremendous frustration for parents. They cause hurt in families. Some studies suggest that the bullying that occurs between siblings is as bad for our children's health as any bullying that might occur outside the home or online.

Kids – please fight some more. It's good for you!

There are, however, some arguments *for* sibling rivalry. Let's address those first, then move to the ways to stop it, because in theory you'll agree with this section but in practice it will drive you mad and you'll just want it all to go away!

Sibling rivalry teaches children important principles. They learn to get along with others, develop empathy, support those they don't necessarily like and even how to argue better. History is full of people in partnerships, whether siblings, office companions or spouses, who bickered constantly and achieved great things, not in spite of their fighting but because of their fighting. Examples include Venus and Serena Williams, whose tennis only got better because of their rivalry. Orville and Wilbur Wright, the forefathers of modern flight, famously argued endlessly as they grappled with how to make a plane fly. Orville stated, 'After long arguments we often found ourselves in the ludicrous position of each having been converted to the other's side with no more agreement than when the discussion began.' John Lennon and Paul McCartney, while not brothers, achieved greatness because of their regular spats over melodies, harmonies, lyrics and instruments. The same can be said for Apple founders Steve Jobs and Steve Wozniak.

Our entire political and legal system, rightly or wrongly, is based on the ability to deal with an adversary effectively. And it all begins in the home.

We do, however, need to be sure that the rivalry, argumentation and conflict is never personally hostile. When it becomes bullying, belittling or a beat-up, we need to step in and teach some basic rules.

First, conflict and debate are different. One is a fight. The other is a challenging conversation where efforts are made to both listen and convince. Second, it's fine to believe that you're right. But it's also important to understand that the other person thinks that they are right, so we should listen to them to understand why they might think that. Third, children (and grown-ups) should learn to acknowledge what their adversary got right. It keeps everyone humble and helps us to focus on learning.

The rest of this chapter will help us deal with those times when these ideas are hard to follow.

Stopping sibling rivalry

i don't remember who said it first but the best way to stop sibling rivalry and sibling squabbles is … to not have siblings.

Too late? Same.

I love what PJ O'Rourke said: 'Anybody can have one kid – but going from one kid to two is like going from owning a dog to running a zoo.'

Have your children ever drawn an imaginary (or real) line down the middle of their room or in the back seat of the car and said, 'You stay on your side or I'll tear your arms off!'?

Have you heard your children whine:

'He's touching me!'

'Make him stop looking at me!'

'She's teasing me!'

My favourite sibling complaint was shared by a tired patient years ago. One of his children complained to their mum:

'Mum, he's breathing my air!'

Preventing sibling conflict is almost impossible, but we can do a handful of things to reduce how often it occurs and how bad it gets. No, you don't need to buy one of everything for each child. Sharing is part of being in a family. Instead, try these tips.

1. **Give individual attention to all of your children**. It will never be quite equal. But when someone needs it, be there for them.

2. When everyone needs attention and individual triage just isn't possible, either **use distraction** or **do something together**.

3. **Be aware of triggers** (hunger, anger, loneliness, tiredness) **and intervene early**. If the children are tired and hungry, keep them separated if you can!

4. **Make sure the big ones don't become parents to the little ones**. 'You're not the boss of me!' means that someone may be over-exerting their authority and parents need to be more present.

5. **Be clear on limits**. 'We are respectful. We speak nicely.'

6. **Avoid smacking**. This models aggression and violence to our children. They're more likely to repeat it.

7. **Teach children to soothe themselves**. Staring at the sky; taking deep, calming breaths; counting back from 1000 in threes; dig a hole in the sandpit to bury your anger, or let it fly away like a kite or dissolve into some water like a tablet; drawing your frustration; listening to music. Each of these ideas can help a child relax.

8. **If you can name it you can tame it**. If you sense a child is becoming frustrated, name it. This will help them know their emotions are normal and can be dealt with positively.

9. **Teach and model empathy.**

Remember that it's tough being a sibling, especially when you're young. Older siblings often ridicule and torment younger siblings. This is painful for anyone. (It's also worth remembering that we often expect more of older siblings, even when they're still very young themselves.)

Why can't we all just get along?

Linus, a character in Charles Schulz's *Peanuts* cartoon, once complained, 'Big [siblings] are the crab grass in the lawn of life.'

Older siblings would beg to differ. As an oldest child, I'm certain it's younger siblings.

But the reality is that being in a family is tough for everyone. Parents and children alike struggle to get along. Parents consistently ask me how they can make their kids treat each other more respectfully, more kindly. 'Why won't they just be nice to each other?'

I often ask those parents how they got along with their siblings as they were growing up. Most acknowledge that they had some challenges.

Next question: now that you're an adult, how are you getting along with your siblings? And how far apart do you live? And how old were you before (if) those relationships started to become more peaceful?

Conflict among siblings is normal. That's because conflict among people is normal. It doesn't mean it's ideal or wonderful. But it is part of being human! We chafe when others do things that we don't understand or like. We feel wounded when words are spoken unkindly. We bristle when they respond to us in a way that feels unfair.

I believe that, so long as it doesn't turn abusive, conflict in sibling relationships can be helpful and important. It's how we learn to set boundaries, be assertive, show compassion and develop respect. It's how we learn to share things as well as experiences. It is sibling conflict – and the way we address it – that teaches us, ultimately, about relationships.

Sibling bonds are like financial bonds. They take a long time to mature. Even with distance and the opportunity to live in separate homes, we often still have sibling struggles.

The vicious circle

One of the most common questions parents ask as they rush into the room to pull their children apart during conflict is:

'Who started it?'

Without fail, each sibling points at the other. The sibling who is most persuasive or most willing to lie wins the conversation and escapes the bulk of their parents' wrath. But invariably, both siblings are reprimanded, and often sent to their rooms 'until you can treat one another nicely'.

> **Parent:** You go to your rooms and think about what you've done.
>
> **Child:** *(walks to room and thinks to self)* Hmmm. I've been a lousy brother. I shouldn't pick on my sister any more. My parents have a point. I think when I'm allowed out of here, I'll be a better human because of this thinking time. I should apologise to everyone and thank my parents for helping me to improve.

It doesn't work like that in real life. When we isolate our children as punishment, they ruminate. The stories they tell themselves create greater difficulties. A child is more likely to say to herself, 'I hate my parents. They don't understand! They think it's all my fault. I always get blamed. It's not fair.'

As they continue to seethe, vengeance becomes a priority. 'As soon as I get out of here and my parents aren't watching, I'm going to get my brother back so bad. He's dead meat.' (Yes, I hate the phrase ... but it's what they say and think.)

In some instances, we may sit down with our children and try to work things out. If our conversation follows the typical pattern, we create a vicious circle that leads to ineffective punishments that often make things worse, not better.

Let's assume we are trying to be as effective as possible, so we start with 'Explain', as the previous chapter described. We decide to go with the advanced parenting practice and so instead of explaining the rules (which we see will be ineffective), we invite our child to explain what is going on for us.

Parent: Why don't you explain things to me so I can understand?

Daughter: He's calling me names and he took my doll and cut its hair, and then he tried to run it over with his bike … and now the dog's eating my doll because he smeared it with dog food.

At this point, some of us choose to stop focusing on 'Explain', ignore 'Explore', and go with 'Explode'! This is unlikely to be helpful.

So we call our son out.

Parent: Your sister has told me you called her names, wrecked her doll and fed it to the dog!

Son: No I didn't.

Parent: Well it looks like you did. Look! Tiger's chewing on the doll right now. And see the hair right there on the floor next to the scissors?

Son: I didn't do anything. Besides, she drank my milkshake while I was playing Minecraft and she said, 'Ner ner ner ner ner' when I got mad at her for it.

Parent: Did you do that to him?

Daughter: No I did not. He told me I could have it and there was none left, and *he* said, 'Ner ner ner ner ner' to *me*!

At this point, chaos resumes and we wonder how to fix the issue. We go around and around inside this vicious circle where each child blames the other for hurt feelings and vengeful behaviour. It looks like this:

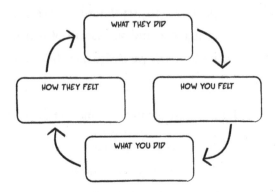

Child One does something and the sibling feels angry, frustrated or upset. Those feelings lead to aggressive or vengeful actions by Child Two towards their sibling. After all, they feel like they're the victim here, and they need to defend themselves by fighting back. They also feel justified in doing what they did because 'she did it to me first'.

When Child Two responds angrily towards the sibling who seems to have started it, that sibling feels angry and, in many cases, now gets to feel like the victim. They feel that they need to fight back. The cycle continues with each sibling getting madder and madder at the other for their worse and worse behaviour.

This vicious circle keeps everyone in what I call BED. BED stands for Blame, Excuse and Denial. We want them to get out of BED and use their OAR. We want them to take Ownership, be Accountable and show Responsibility.

But because our usual response to our children is based on 'who started it?' and 'why are you kids doing this?', we keep them in a vicious circle of Blame, Excuse and Denial. They lie, point fingers at one another and do all they can to escape the worn-out, exasperated parent who just wants to know why they can't get along. The most persuasive one gets the other one in the most trouble, and no one really learns anything except that life is unfair.

Getting out of the vicious circle

So how do we change the conversation and help siblings work things out?

My belief is that no matter how hard we try, we will always have at least some challenges here. Children are people, too. And this means that they will have conflict and aggravations together. It is unavoidable.

The way we respond to their irritations and skirmishes can impact the outcomes for our children and family. But it also influences the skills they learn for getting along. I suggest the following.

First, always be calmer than your children. Call through the door that your child is sitting against in order to block your entry. Invite the two children to sit at the table with you.

Then, on a piece of paper draw the first box in the vicious circle:

Pick one of the two children and describe your understanding of what has occurred. (I typically choose the child who feels most aggrieved.) Note: never ask questions you already know the answer to. Otherwise you'll have to get the children in trouble for lying as well! Instead, just state what you know, so there's no chance for someone to misrepresent the situation.

To continue with the example above, your daughter begins to tell you how her big brother has upset her and destroyed her doll. Draw the box above and start writing down all of the things she tells you.

Your son will protest.

Son: Yeah, well, she ...

Gently let him know that it's time to listen just now, but that you'll give him a chance to talk in a moment.

Now draw the second box like this:

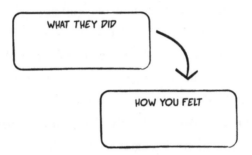

Ask your daughter how that made her feel. She'll say things like, 'I felt upset and angry and worried.' Write those responses into the box. At this stage, you are still only talking to the upset child. Your other child may wish to interject. Stay calm and remind him that he'll be able to share some things soon.

Next, draw the third box and ask your daughter how she responded to her brother's anger. Write those ideas down in the next box.

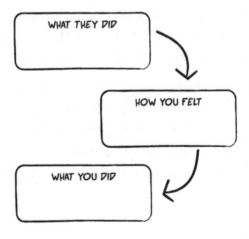

Finally, draw the fourth box and ask your daughter, 'How did he feel when you did this?'

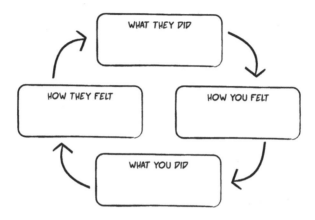

This is where the magic begins. To this point, things feel like any standard 'he said, she said' argument. But now we are focused on *perspective* and *empathy*. Your daughter has been doing all the talking. She's been allowed to live in Blame, Excuse and Denial for the first three boxes. Now, as she begins to contemplate how *her* actions have affected her brother, she has to recognise the responsibility she has for her brother's feelings. She becomes accountable. Write down the things she identifies her brother has felt.

Something interesting will often happen here. As her brother hears your little girl describe his feelings, he will feel understood. He will lose the desire to defend himself and accuse his sister.

Three critical questions

Check with your children and make sure the four boxes represent their view of things. Then, draw arrows between them and ask three questions:

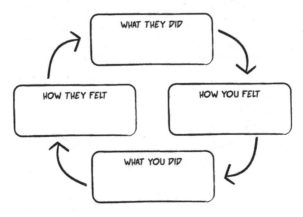

1. Who started it?

In a perfect world your children will identify that no one has really started it and that they are both responsible for it. Usually, however, this is not what happens. They still point fingers at one another. That's fine, because the purpose of this question is to make the following point:

It doesn't matter who started it. What matters most are the answers to the following two questions.

2. Who is contributing to it?

Next, we ask our children, 'Who is contributing to this challenging situation?' Even a four-year-old can tell that she is contributing to this issue. The central thing we are looking for here is ownership. If there is conflict, both people involved in that conflict are contributing to it. The vicious circle depicts this. Regardless of 'who started it', both contribute as soon as there is retaliation or negative response.

Parent: You're both pretty upset with each other. I can see that. I'm not interested in who started it. I'm interested in who is contributing to it. And it seems like you both are to some extent. Fair enough?

(Silent nods from the children.)

3. Who is responsible for making things better?

The most important question we ask is question three. This promotes children's use of their OARs. They Own the solution and become Accountable for improving things. Their empathy for one another makes them want to behave Responsibly.

Parent: So where do we go from here? What do you think we need to do to make things work again?

At this point, we have spent considerable time working through our three Es, but in a completely different way that emphasises empathy and perspective. Our travels through the vicious circle highlight both Explain and Explore – but the children are doing most of the work. This means that their brains are working far harder (and more effectively) than they might if we were doing all of the lecturing.

And the Empowerment comes as we invite our children to find ways to make things right.

I asked my mentor, Professor of Family Life Dr H Wallace Goddard, to offer his best tips for responding to sibling conflict. He provided them here to help you guide your children using the example of a boy playing with his Lego when his younger sister interrupts and breaks something. He acts out in anger, pushing her and calling her names.

1. **Engage your son in a gentle way**. Harsh approaches arouse anxiety and block learning. When we are upset, we are not able to parent effectively. We may need to take time out to get peaceful. If a situation requires immediate action, we might invite our children to also take a moment to compose themselves somewhere safe to prepare for a productive dialogue. It is important to get his attention without arousing fear: 'Son, we need to talk. Your sister is very upset by the way you treated her.'

2. **Give your child credit for anything you can**. 'I'm sure you didn't intend to hurt your sister's feelings.' We are often tempted to magnify the misdeeds in order to get our children to take our message seriously. But when we appreciate their good intentions and sincere striving, we are more likely to find common ground.

3. **Show that you understand your son's point of view**. 'You just wanted to build without being distracted or interrupted.' Compassion is the key to connecting. When accusation rather than compassion is in our hearts, we alienate. When, in contrast, I see from the child's point of view, I am able to guide effectively. Compassion is the heart of the healer's art.

4. **Draw the child's attention to the distress of the victim**. 'When you ordered your sister to leave you alone, she felt sad. She felt that you don't like to have her around.'
   There are really two parts to this step. We inform our child's mind *and* our child's heart. We invite the child to learn his sister's point of view: 'I think your sister just wanted to be with you.'

We also train our children's hearts. This is delicate work! Heart surgery cannot be done with sledgehammers. Rather, we gently invite our children to feel love and compassion for their siblings. 'You might not know that your sister looks up to you. She wants to be like you. I hope you can find a way for her to be with you while still accomplishing the things you set out to do.'

The objective in this approach is not for your son to be sunk in guilt but to be stirred to empathy and compassion. When we use harsh approaches with our children, they focus on their own distress and are likely to become stubborn and defensive. That's not what we want. We want to help our children get outside their view of their own needs and be able to see the needs of others.

We cannot rush this process. When the child protests, 'But she is the one who messed up my work!' we do not have to argue. We return to the third step, showing understanding for his point of view: 'It's pretty frustrating, isn't it!' When the child feels genuinely understood, then he is ready to learn in his mind and in his heart.

Help the child to feel genuine compassion for the one he has hurt. If we want our child to show compassion, we must model compassion. Naturally, your child will resist your challenge: 'She can't start grabbing Legos when I'm building something.' We can argue that he shouldn't be so unkind to his sister. And he will argue with us about his sister's misdeeds. Rather than squabbling with the boy, we can show empathy: 'It's hard when you're in the middle of a project and she interrupts you or starts using your Legos.' He does, after all, have a valid point. When we show him compassion, he is more able to show compassion for his sister. Incidentally, it may take several rounds of expressing understanding and compassion before he is ready to show compassion for his sister. Healing through compassion takes time.

5. **Once the child feels understood** (as evidenced by being calm and peaceful), then we can **help the child think of a way to make repairs**. 'How could we help your sister feel loved and welcome without messing up your project?'

   When hearts are right, creativity can rule. 'Maybe I could help her build a house,' or 'I could provide her with some of the blocks.' It is a joyous surprise when children feel safe and loved and naturally love and serve each other.

Any parent might reasonably protest that this process takes a lot of time. You're right! Parenting is not quick, simple or convenient. Parenting is a large and continuing sacrifice. Yet an hour spent teaching them in their youth can save years of conflict, struggle and waywardness.

Of course, this approach is not the perfect one in all circumstances. When a child is in danger, action is needed more than instruction. When a child is so tired or upset that reasoning is not possible, some time for calming is called for. When a child holds a parent hostage – requiring them to prove their point to the child's satisfaction – this is not the right approach.

The remarkable power of empathy

We might add a fourth E to this conversation. It is not so much a part of the process as it is an outcome of the process. That E is Empathy.

The central way to promote positive relationships is to help our children understand how their siblings feel, and see the world through their eyes. We do this best by example. Our conversation about the vicious circle reinforces an empathetic perspective.

In his book *Originals*, Adam Grant, a psychology professor in the USA, wrote about a study comparing non-Jews who risked their lives to save Jewish neighbours in World War II with those who didn't. The researchers focused on what children were told by their parents. Those who were involved in rescuing gave 'explanations of why behaviours are inappropriate, often with reference to their consequences for others'. The rescuers' parents encouraged their children to consider the impact of their actions on others. Those who stood by and watched focused on enforcing compliance with the rules for their own sake.

When we focus on the other child, we promote empathy and a moral compass. Our children want to help, not hurt.

> **Parent:** When you tease your sister, how does it make her feel?
>
> **Child:** Bad.
>
> **Parent:** It sure does. What can we do to make her feel better?

When we go crazy at our kids, they miss our message and they learn to fear us. In serious cases, we damage them. When we let things slide, they miss our message and they ignore us. This means we aren't parenting.

When we get the balance 'just right' (not too harsh, not too soft), we engage them emotionally by getting them to focus on the other person and their feelings. We engage them mentally by asking them to explain what they observe. Then we ask them to come up with good ways to act.

This approach means that we maintain a good relationship with them, and we get an important message through.

When my eldest was three, she hurt her baby sister. I asked, 'How did Abbie feel when you did that?' Her reply: 'Sad.' I asked, 'What is the best way to help her feel good?' And my eldest walked to her sister and hugged her.

Empathy and perspective will be far better teachers than a screaming parent, the loss of a privilege or the back of your hand. The vicious circle, combined with the principles of understanding outlined in Chapter 3, emphasise how empathy can help.

Forcing children to apologise

When our children treat one another badly, parents often demand that a child apologise for their behaviour. Usually we expect that the apology will be instant! But we shouldn't insist on making things happen fast. Sometimes our children may need some time to consider the best way to make things better.

Our focus should be on helping, not hurting. We want progress, not perfection. When we give our children space, they come to their own conclusions about good ways to treat one another. When we demand they conform to our conclusions, they resist.

A former neighbour of mine, Elizabeth (not her real name), thinks apologies need to be taught like manners. When a child forgets to say 'Please' or 'Thank you', we instantly remind them to use their manners. Elizabeth suggests that the same needs to occur with apologies. When a child does something that requires an 'I'm sorry', parents should expect it right there and then – while the situation is still going.

As an example, if Elizabeth's two children, Will and Chloe, are fighting, and three-year-old Will hits Chloe (aged five), Elizabeth will separate them and comfort Chloe. She will then require Will to 'say sorry'. Chloe will then be asked to say, 'Thank you for saying sorry.'

Elizabeth suggests that to respond to an apology with 'It's okay' is wrong, because when people do the wrong thing it's not okay.

Elizabeth told me, 'I definitely demand that the children apologise in the moment. I'll do it nicely, but the kids need to know they're not getting anything – we don't move beyond this situation – until they give an appropriate apology.' Elizabeth acknowledges that sometimes her children are in tears before they actually apologise, but she's okay with that.

When I asked her why she feels so strongly about forcing children to apologise, Elizabeth told me that many of her clients in relationship therapy never said sorry. 'It's not part of their vocabulary. Regardless of what they've done wrong, they don't say those words. They show they're sorry by buying things and making it up in other ways. But the words never come.'

I feel differently. I believe that children should be taught and encouraged to apologise, but not through force. Apologies will come *naturally* when they feel peaceful and their empathy is activated.

Children, like adults, don't want to say sorry when they feel they have to. When it's forced, it feels inauthentic and meaningless. It is spat across the room with no contrition. And it isn't really an apology. Even when the apology is delivered the way we want it delivered – politely – there is still no meaning behind it.

I suggest that children be asked to apologise, but it's unlikely that it will mean anything 'in the moment'. If the apology is not good enough, my recommendation is to get out of the moment. Tend to hurt children and ensure they're okay. Then wait until the child who 'needs to apologise' is willing to talk about what happened.

They're unlikely to want to talk, so I suggest we sit with them, hug them and assure them they're not in trouble. We just need to talk. When they feel safe, talk about the issue and ask them to consider how it felt from the injured person's perspective. There are almost always two sides to a story. They may have felt justified in their actions (though of course, in the case of violence, there is never adequate justification). Rather than apportioning blame, we need to simply help them recognise that they hurt someone or did wrong. Once they can see that their actions hurt them, we should ask them, 'What is the right thing to do now?'

TEACHING CHILDREN TO APOLOGISE WELL

I believe every apology should contain four elements:

1. I'm sorry.

2. I know that what I did hurt you (or whatever the outcome of the action was).

3. What I did was wrong.

4. Will you forgive me?

As we talk with our children, we can help them to understand that these elements make up a full apology.

When a person asks for forgiveness, the injured party doesn't have to say, 'That's okay,' or even 'Thanks for the apology.' Instead, they simply say, 'Yes, I forgive you'. (And no, forgiveness right there and then is *not* a given.)

Elizabeth and I disagree on the timing of the apology. Elizabeth says it should be right now. I say do it when it can be done sincerely.

We disagree on whether we should force our child to apologise. I say, 'No way.' Elizabeth says, 'Definitely.'

Elizabeth and I share the belief that children should learn to apologise in honest and sincere ways, and that parents need to be good examples of seeking forgiveness.

Every child (and adult) makes mistakes. Saying sorry for those mistakes matters, but morality takes a long time to develop. Rather than rushing it and forcing apologies, I believe we should be gentle in the way we encourage empathy, and help our children to learn what a true apology is so they can offer them meaningfully. Ultimately, forced apologies train children to say things that they don't mean. That is, forced apologies teach children to lie.

(Sorry Elizabeth!)

Getting along with others

This chapter is about siblings not getting along. But the truth is, we all struggle to get along with others. Sometimes we bicker and argue with other adults, including our own parents, siblings or partner. Other times we even get into arguments with our children. A scary stat: according to Dr John Gottman's research, parents are the ones who start 75 per cent of fights with children. They pick up on those topics that make children feel challenged or defensive. They say, 'So what happened with the teacher at school today?' Or, 'Why didn't you do what you were told this afternoon after school? You have a list to follow. You know what we expect. What's going on?' While conversational enquiry is great, some questions provoke defensiveness and stonewalling in children. Some questions lead to arguments and frustration. Parents' desire to correct can all-too-often turn dinner into difficulty.

That is, we are the ones who respond to our children's challenging behaviour in ways the promote conflict.

Every parent will say, 'Well, if they did the right thing I wouldn't need to correct them.' That is an understandable position. But when we commence correcting our children in ways that make them feel bad, we create our own vicious circle with them. In essence, we're saying, 'But, but, but I didn't start it.'

We need to get out of BED (Blame, Excuse and Denial) and use our OAR (Ownership, Accountability and Responsibility). Own it. It doesn't matter who started it. All that matters is who contributes to it and who is going to be responsible for stopping it. We have the skills to deal with this. The first several chapters of this book provide a useful guide. And we actually *can* do it. For example, when the child who is challenging is not our child, we generally behave with great maturity. We remain in control, poised and patient. Similarly, when we have an audience, we keep it together and remain grown up. One mum emailed me and said, 'I just pretend you're in the room watching me parent. It's changed everything!'

Take-home message

Every parent with more than one child – in fact, every human in a relationship – will experience some form of conflict. This can be good. Conflict allows us to re-examine habits and priorities, and gives us the possibility of progress. But it can be bad if we don't use it to improve.

The heart of resolving conflict between our children, or between any humans, is empathy. *Empathy is the key.* When a child can gain insight into the reasons their siblings behave the way they do, they may recognise the part they have played in the problem. As they see the impact *they* have on others (and vice versa), they feel empathy and make changes that are much longer lasting than changes that are forced upon them by powerful parents.

6

Discovering the self

'I've got a question for you', the cab driver stated expectantly. I was on my way to give a talk about parenting. He had asked where I was going and why, and his eyes lit up when he found out what I do for work.

I had emails to respond to. I had a call or two to make. But I love to talk parenting so I smiled and said, 'Go for it. What's your question?'

'How do I make sure my son becomes a pilot?'

I was surprised by this question. Most of the time I'm asked about discipline, getting kids off screens and the other day-to-day minutiae of parenting power struggles. This was a direct question about how a dad could seemingly enforce or manipulate his son into a career that he may or may not want to pursue.

The cabbie, a lovely bloke named Mohammad, was well meaning. He obviously loved his son and wanted the best for him. But I was uncomfortable with what he was asking. What if his son didn't want to become a pilot? What if this was just an ambitious (and possibly controlling) father setting unfair or unrealistic expectations on his son? What happens if his son fails? These and other questions raced through my head as I considered how to respond to him politely but clearly.

Through this taxi driver's eyes, being a pilot was a symbol of success. It would mean that his son was living a successful life, and it would also mean that *he* had been a successful father. We talked about this. But would it really matter what career choices his son made? (Would his son even have a choice?)

Eventually I suggested: 'My sense is that who your son becomes – that is, the character your son develops – will be far more important to his happiness in life than what he becomes in a professional sense. Additionally, your job is not to make him a pilot, but instead to help him become who and what he wants to be.'

As parents, many of us spend far too much time focused on values like ambition, income and other outward symbols of success. Yet these things do not make us happy. The central lie of our entire society is that income, status and 'success' lead to happiness. But dozens of studies conducted by multiple research groups across different countries and over several decades have found that once the rent or mortgage is covered, food is in our fridge and we have the basics taken care of, money does not make us happier.

I suggested to Mohammad that focusing on building values like honesty, compassion and kindness might serve his son better and help him lead a happier, more fulfilling life. 'If your son is a pilot but is not a person of character, will he be successful? Or what about if he becomes a taxi driver like you, but he is a good man, loves his family and works hard? What would make him happier? Or you?'

But the driver was sceptical. I shifted perspectives.

'When you look at your dad, do you see him as a professional or as a person?' I asked him. He explained that his father lived in India, and that he had very little money. 'And do you value him less because he is poor?'

'No, of course not. He is my father,' he replied.

'Do you feel your son is going to think poorly of you because you drive a taxi?'

The driver was thoughtful, and he responded with honest vulnerability.

'No. I think I am the one who thinks poorly of me. He will see me as his dad in the same way that I see my father.'

'So what kind of a dad do you want to be?' We talked about whether it was more important to be a father who was rich financially, or a father who possessed a rich character. We discussed whether it was more important to be a pushy parent or one who let his children discover themselves.

'Your job as a father is to help your son become the man he is supposed to be. That may or may not involve him flying planes for a living. It is up to you to help him find that inbuilt potential for excellence that is inside him – that thing that lights him up – and encourage him to pursue it with vigour. And it is up to you to help him to become a person of character.'

In the workshops that I run around the country, I often ask parents what they want most for their children. The first responses are almost always, 'I want them to be happy. I want them to have a good life.'

While enjoying financial successes and career status may help them to be happy and live good lives (and there are many people for whom this is true), this cannot – this must not – be the measure of our children's success in life or our success as parents.

Character and financial success are not mutually exclusive. We can have both. But whereas life can be wonderfully fulfilling if we have character without the status and success that society tells us is so important, it almost certainly will not be so fulfilling if we have the success but not the character to accompany it.

What are the character traits that make a person truly successful? Kindness, respect, integrity, service to others, curiosity, compassion, understanding, a desire for excellence. There are attributes like perseverance, creativity, modesty and gratitude. Then there's the vital ability to recognise our mistakes and grow from them.

The word 'character' originally referred to a stamping tool, used to imprint a symbol onto a surface. I love that imagery. When we stamp something in this way we make it permanent. These characteristics aren't superficial practices we pull out from time to time in order to manipulate someone. Instead, they are stamped on us – or, more rightly, in us.

As we focus on developing and building these attributes, we will help our children grow into people of character. And these attributes will lead them to lives that are less about status and success, and more about making a difference. They'll discover their best selves and contribute positively wherever their strengths lie.

'How will you feel about your son if he doesn't become a pilot? Will you feel that he is a failure? Will you see him as unsuccessful?'

'Of course not.'

'How will he feel about himself if you continually push him to be a pilot but he never quite gets there? Or perhaps he decides to do something else?'

The cabbie was thoughtful. 'He might feel like he is a failure. Or that he has disappointed me.'

I felt like I had got through to Mohammad. His responses had been thoughtful. He seemed to be open to the ideas we discussed. An obvious question occurred to me.

'By the way,' I asked him, 'does your son want to become a pilot?'

'I'm not really sure. I just really want him to be one.'

'Oh. Okay. How old is your son?'

'He's two months old.'

I'm glad we had this conversation when we did.

Force creates resistance

Anonymous street artist and satirist Banksy said, 'A lot of parents will do anything for their children, except let them be themselves.'

In some cases, we may be right to dig in and make demands. We know that it is best that they eat their vegetables, do their schoolwork and get enough sleep. But force creates resistance. The harder we push our children to conform, the more they want to rebel. Our demands give them something to push against.

From the time that they become toddlers, we start placing limits on our children's behaviour. (Some parents start even earlier.) This is usually important and appropriate, but at times we become too controlling. As control increases, so does our child's resistance. They want to rebel and react against our control. They want autonomy. While inconvenient, this reaction is healthy and normal. In fact, resistance to parental authority is associated with psychological autonomy: a key marker of wellbeing. If you're *that* parent who is always talking about how independent and defiant and 'strong-willed' your little ones are, you can take some comfort in your challenging experiences: research shows that defiant toddlers develop better.

We must acknowledge that our children's defiance and resistance are inconvenient. Many of us are like Darth Vader – we want to crush the resistance and create an empire where our minions follow us with blind conformity. But this is unhelpful for our children's development. It can be hard for us to encourage our children to 'be who they really are' when they aren't allowed to make any decisions. Worse still, they cannot discover who they really are when the decisions they are making are all reactions to our assertions of power. In an almost perverse perfection, however, our limits are essential for our children to figure out who they really are. They actually *need* something to push against. Pushing against things is how we build strength physically, mentally and psychologically.

We, as parents, naturally provide the perfect platform for our children to become who they really are as we give them limits to test themselves against. We metaphorically become a boulder our children can struggle with. The power in this perfect plan is that we can be a safe place for them to experience this fight.

The way we work through this process – or perhaps struggle or tussle might be better words – has a profound impact on whether our children really become who they are capable of becoming. When we use our formidable advantage over our children to win every argument, force every issue and dominate, they never really form their own identity. They become who they are told to become.

John B Watson, a 'founding father' of modern psychology, stated, 'Give me a dozen healthy infants, well-formed, and my own specified world to bring them up in and I'll guarantee to take any one at random and train him to become any type of specialist I might select – doctor, lawyer, artist, merchant-chief and, yes, even beggar-man and thief, regardless of his talents, penchants, tendencies, abilities, vocations and race of his ancestors.'

Watson's shadow looms large in many families as parents try to make their children into their preferred version of success. (The film *Dead Poets Society* may be a powerful pop-culture example of this approach taken to a tragic conclusion. It's a remarkable example of just how badly wrong such parenting can go in the worst of circumstances.)

Something about that force and manipulation feels wrong – though it is enticing because we want the best for our children, and making them conform, we are sure, means we will get what we want. After all, my taxi driver was keen on making his son's career decisions for him. Many parents want their children to become something other than who/what they are. But is this what is best for them? Sometimes, perhaps. Let's acknowledge that some children really do want something that will be bad for them. But most of the time, manipulating them may leave them feeling controlled and unfulfilled. Our aim is not to manipulate them, but to guide them to flourish and thrive.

The identity quest

What do we mean when we talk about letting our children be 'themselves'?

I'm going to suggest four specific understandings that can help our children become who they 'really' are. First, we need to help them understand themselves. Second, we assist them to discover that thing that lights them up and makes them come alive – their strengths: their *spark*. Third, we guide them to think for themselves rather than following the crowd. Fourth, we get out of their way, trust them, and provide them with autonomy.

Who am I really?

The quest to find out who we really are lasts a lifetime. Children typically begin thinking about who they are in their late tweens, but we plant the seeds of identity much younger. For any child (or parent) who has watched Disney movies, the underlying theme of almost all of them relates to a quest of self-discovery. Simba left his home and spent years making foolish and selfish decisions before his father, Mufasa, appeared to him in a vision and told him to 'Remember who you are.'

Aladdin had a genie who asked him to look inside himself and discover whether he might be more than just a 'street rat', and in the process, eventually learn about living with integrity. Merida (in the movie *Brave*) is another example of a character our children love who is discovering who she really is. Elsa and Anna in *Frozen*, Marlin and Nemo, Woody and Buzz: each are examples of the quest to find out who we are, what stuff we're made of and where we belong.

The Disney film *Moana* even has the lyrics that a whole village sings: 'We know who we are!'

In every case, these fictional characters discover who they are by encountering hardship and challenge, and overcoming it by drawing on their reservoirs of resilience. They lean on their past, their culture, their friends and their family. The same applies for our children.

When they are young and they have troubles, we cocoon them and support them. As they mature, we start to tell them stories about how we got through similar challenges. (We don't support them by preaching.) They learn from grandparents and aunts or uncles. They develop a sense of family identity. The older they become, the more we work with them to help them discover who they are. (I'll describe how we do this later in this Chapter.)

In *9 Ways to a Resilient Child*, I emphasised research by Professor Marshall Duke of Emory University in the USA, which showed that for children who had a strong sense of family identity, resilience was significantly higher than for children who didn't really know where they belonged or where they came from. Teaching our children about our family history and identity provides them with the foundations for their own identity. It puts them on the path of healthy self-discovery.

What lights you up?

Have you noticed that your child is energised, thrilled and excited by some things but lackadaisical about, bored by or uninterested in others?

Each of our children has unique talents, strengths and gifts. Helping them to discover those things that *spark* delight and enthusiasm inside themselves, and developing those things over time, will help them to discover themselves.

Pete and Natalie are parents to Max. Early on, Max discovered science. Pete and Natalie fostered this interest by providing Max with resources, access to YouTube science channels, and time together developing this interest and learning together. Max *loves* science and regularly creates his own science projects. His curiosity and inquisitiveness are part of who he is and as he has developed competence in science, his confidence has grown and that spark has lit a fire that will not be diminished.

When our children find *that thing* that feels so good to them, it becomes a part of their identity. They discover themselves and they discover things that may bring them joy throughout their lives. It provides purpose and meaning.

We may want them to discover guitar and they may choose opera. We may want them to follow our passion for netball or rugby and they may want to pursue drama and the arts. Our focus needs to be on what lights them up, and not what we want them to be lit up with.

As we identify our children's strengths, we may find that there are both *things that they perform well in*, and *characteristics that appear to come naturally to them*. Encouraging our children to *do* things that make them feel good is easy. Encouraging them to *be* those attributes can be more challenging.

Parents can be a social mirror for their children: 'I love watching how you respond to people who are hurting.' 'I love the way you light up when you are discovering new things.' Pointing out these attributes can go a long way to helping children discover who they are, and what lights them up.

Don't follow the crowd

Over the past several decades, fascinating studies have shown that as humans, we are an ultra-social species. We see what others are doing and we want to belong so badly that we will choose to give up our own identity to be a part of the crowd.

In his classic psychology studies from the 1950s, Solomon Asch found that people would say things that they *knew* were blatantly wrong in order to be accepted. In his studies, a participant entered a room where there were up to 11 other people. Each looked at three parallel lines. The lines were of different lengths. The differences were obvious. A fourth line was shown to the people in the room and they were asked to judge which of the three lines was the same length as the fourth line. The first 11 people would intentionally say the wrong thing (because they were conspiring with the experimenter to see what the real participant would say). In close to 40 per cent of cases, the participant would reluctantly and uneasily agree that they were right when it was obvious that they weren't. What would your kids say or do? What would *you* say or do? Are we following the path of least resistance? Are we bowing down to the god of Popular Opinion? Or do we know who we are?

Stanley Milgram is another psychology researcher who shocked the world with his obedience studies from the 1960s. He found that simply telling people to do something unethical was enough to have them abandon their morality (reluctantly and under pressure) to follow his instructions. His participants believed that they were electrocuting another participant to death, and two-thirds of them carried out his instructions anyway. The shocks weren't real, but the participants didn't know this. And so they delivered these shocks over and over again. They did so reluctantly, remorsefully and repeatedly. Again, what would you and your kids do? Stand for what's right because you know who you are?

Or follow the crowd, be obedient and go down a path you don't want to because of the pressure?

Study after study shows that our children follow the crowd under fairly normal conditions. They succumb to peer pressure. They are not willing to think independently if it may cause them to stand alone.

We can support our children to be themselves by encouraging independent thought. To help our children become who they really are, I love the idea of taking a proactive approach where we play with hypotheticals. We can sit with our child in the car or at bedtime and ask, 'What would you do in this instance? Why? What other ideas do you have?' We can ask them, 'What if everyone else was doing this? What would you do?'

As we take our children through challenging scenarios in the safety of our presence, they can prepare for similar scenarios that might occur without us being there. And we can adapt real-life circumstances for pre-arming conversations as well.

> **Parent:** You're at school and someone in the playground starts taunting, teasing and name-calling another student. What do you do? What if it's not someone you know? What if they're bigger than you? What if it's your best friend who is doing the bullying?

> **Parent:** You're at a sleepover party and one of the other kids starts looking up rude words on the iPad. What do you do? Should you just pretend to be asleep? Or should you leave the room? Would it be right or wrong to tell a parent? What if the parents are people you don't know well and they're in bed and asleep?

> **Parent:** Your sister says something nasty to you. What's the best thing to do?

Each time your child experiences a challenge, it is an opportunity to talk with them about who they really are. We can invite them to act on what they know to be right and to think for themselves, even when they have to stand alone *or against others*.

If our child does something that shows a lack of humanity, purpose or identity, we can ask them about that experience. How did it feel for them? How did it feel for others? How might it have affected them? This questioning without judgement, but rather out of curiosity, taps into both a cognitive and affective awareness, and increases the likelihood of an internalised sense of morality. It promotes perspective-taking and empathy.

Helping our children discover who they really are means we teach them to be strong enough to take a stand on an issue or principle, even when no one else will. It's about teaching them that they can be both strong and caring.

These dilemmas may not relate to the decisions our children will make in determining their career. But they go a long way to helping our children develop an understanding of who they really are, and being true to themselves. Such moral conviction allows them to make choices without the noise of the crowd – or parents – interfering with their decisions. And this *will* impact on the decisions they make in their careers, whatever they choose.

Evidence indicates that pre-arming our children helps them develop a strong sense of morality and empathy. This is related to high levels of pro-social behaviour. They treat others well. They are kind. They are compassionate. They stand up for what they believe in.

As they get older, we can start to *defer* decisions to them. When they act in ways that build our trust we say to them, 'I'll leave that up to you,' or, 'You decide this time.' This allows our children to act based on their internal compass – their growing sense of right.

Decisions to defer should be based on maturity and development. We don't tell our 11-year-old that it's up to her whether she drives to the shops or walks there instead. Nor do we invite our six-year-old to get the ice-cream out of the freezer for breakfast if that's what she really wants. (Unless it's on pancakes with lots of other goodies as well!)

It's important to note that giving up, sighing and hoisting the white flag of surrender to our children is completely different to deference. Deference is accompanied by pre-arming conversations, perspective-taking discussions, careful consideration of the options a child might have in front of them and the child's readiness to handle the consequences of their decision. When the parent believes that the child understands the issue and then defers a decision to the child, outcomes are going to be better than, 'Hmph. You decide,' followed by a shrug.

To help our children discover who they really are, we teach them that the crowd can be wrong. We encourage them to think for themselves by giving them hypotheticals that help them to identify their values, and then by deferring decisions to them. When they make mistakes, we don't criticise. We learn together. This allows them to focus on their deeply held values, live with purpose and have confidence in their decisions. And they discover, as Augustine of Hippo said, that 'Right is right, even if no one is doing it, and wrong is wrong, even if everyone is doing it.'

Give them space

Malala Yousafzai is a globally recognised rebel who knew what she stood for. She was born in north-western Pakistan, where her father ran several schools. Despite Taliban directives that girls should not be educated, Ziauddin Yousafzai encouraged his daughter to receive an education. Malala blogged about her experience as a schoolgirl in a Taliban-run location and gained worldwide attention.

On 9 October 2012, a gunman stopped her school bus and asked which of the children inside was Malala. Friends unintentionally looked at her, betraying her identity. Malala was shot in the head. With medical help and eventually a flight to the UK, she miraculously survived. Today, Malala is the youngest ever Nobel Prize laureate, and a vocal campaigner for girls' education around the world.

In an interview about how he was able to raise such a fierce young woman, Malala's father, Ziauddin, said the following.

> People ask me, what is special in my mentorship which has made Malala so bold and so courageous and so vocal and so poised? I tell them don't ask me what I did. Ask me what I did not do. I did not clip her wings, and that's all.

Malala's story is exceptional in every sense. Our children might also make a difference by being willing to stand out. Whether they stop a bully, start a non-profit that benefits others, make life fairer for others or simply live a life of deep personal integrity, knowing who they really are and living in harmony with that knowledge will be central to their discovery. And being pushed into a certain career – or having their life dictated to them by a well-meaning but controlling parent – is unlikely to help them make that impact.

It can be hard to step back and let our children make decisions for themselves. Yet that is how they discover who they are. It can be agonising to watch them make stupid mistakes. Yet that, too, is how they discover how to make good decisions. When we sensitively and patiently work with them and help them to learn to make better decisions next time using the ideas in this chapter, we can then invite them to try again. 'I see you made a poor decision this time. I think you've learned from it. Let's see if I give you another chance, whether you can do it better.'

Raising children who know who they are is hard work – and it's a long game. A child between two and seven will have little interest in knowing or desire to know who she is. She doesn't care — and that's fine. We build a sense of family identity in those years. From the time our children can think logically, however, we can begin these processes and guide them towards discovering who they (and their family) are, tapping into what they love and independent thinking. Then we give them space to discover themselves. From time to time our children will rebel against us. They'll make poor decisions. We learn about ourselves in those moments. And we help them to learn about themselves as well.

As I sat in the taxi in Melbourne that night and spoke with Mohammad, we agreed that the work our children do does *not* define who they are. It may influence their identity, but the person they are stands independent of their work. What ultimately mattered to Mohammad was that his son would grow up knowing about the strong values of his mother and father, and his grandparents, and that these values would guide him as he discovered who he was.

Take-home message

Helping our children to become who they really are is a challenge. It requires teaching them about their past, tapping into that authentic potential for excellence that is inside them and makes them strong, supporting them to have the courage and capacity to stand alone and then trusting that the process will be enough. When we are willing to do these things and then step back in trust and faith, our children can then find out for themselves who they are.

Finding a balance with technology

Ever been a long trip in the car with the kids? I'm talking anything longer than about 30 minutes. If you're like most Aussie families, these 'longer' trips mean the kids will ask for (or automatically be given) the iPhone or the iPad to keep them amused. When I was a kid we didn't have iPhones and iPads – we only had iSpy.

Me: Umm ... I spy with my little eye, something beginning with 'T'.

Dad: Tree.

Me: Oh! That's not fair.

Dad: Okay ... go again.

Me: *(being really, really tricky)* I spy with my little eye something beginning with 'E'.

Dad: *(after three minutes, 18 guesses and a remarkable amount of patience)* I give up.

Me: Excelerator.

Dad: Uhhh ... it's accelerator. It starts with 'A'.

We've tried to play I Spy with our kids. They have two guesses and then complain. 'This is boring. It's too hard. Can I have an iPad?' (In fairness, as parents we get pretty bored with it too, and the iPad means the kids are occupied while the parents talk.)

I love telling my children how tough I had it growing up compared to the extraordinary ease that today's generation enjoys. My kids ask me about the 'olden days' all the time. I tell them I wasn't born back then, but they don't believe me.

> **Me:** Back when I was a kid, we had to get up and walk over to the TV to change the channel.

> **Me:** Back when I was a kid, we had these things called encyclopaedias. There was no Google. If you didn't know something, you had to go to the library and look for the answer in a *book*.

> **Me:** Back when I was a kid, if I wanted to hear my favourite song, I had to sit by the radio and wait for it. Then I'd press *play* and *record* on my cassette player to record the song so I could listen to it whenever I wanted. And fast-forwarding and rewinding was time-consuming and inaccurate.

I wonder what our children are going to tell their children about life in the 2000s.

> **Them:** Back when I was a kid, I had to wait until Year 7 before I got a phone, and the wifi was so bad that we were lucky to get four MBPS. I couldn't even get wifi in my bedroom! I had to sit in the living room. And all I ever heard from my parents was, 'Get off that darned screen!'

Are screens really the enemy?

Screens have created a moral panic among parents. When we talk about devices, phones, tablets or anything else that possesses a screen, judgements are made. We're 'good' parents if we *minimise* screen time. We are 'bad' parents if we allow *too much* screen time.

Ours is the first generation having to seriously deal with the screen tsunami that has swept over society. And we are dealing with concerns our parents could never have considered. When I got my first camera my parents didn't need to sit me down and say, 'Justin, don't take pictures of your privates and send them to everyone!' I mean, who was going to take photos like that and take the film into the local photo shop and have it developed? With accessibility to screens, all of that has changed – and children are being impacted at younger and younger ages. The kicker is this: too many parents simply don't know what to do.

A mum emailing me:

> I'm worried my child is addicted to her iPad. She's seven and is always on it. I asked her when she was hopping off to clean her room, she didn't even look up. She just said, 'In 16 per cent.'

Another mum emailing:

> My 11-year-old daughter takes her laptop into the bathroom with her. She watches episodes of her favourite shows while she has a shower or bath. She even takes the charger in so she can stay in longer without her devices dying. Help. What do I do?

The problem seems to be so worrisome that tech-preneurs in Silicon Valley are reported to insist that their children attend schools and kindergartens where there is *zero* tech available for their children. They limit and even eliminate their kids' exposure to the precise products they peddle to people around the world.

In 2016, Bill Gates told reporters that he doesn't believe any child under the age of 14 should be allowed a telephone – primarily because of the excessive screen time it promotes. Some families have taken this even further, with guidelines of no screens before the age of ten and no phones until the kids can pay for them without parental help!

The morality and guilt around screens and device usage is tremendous. Countless blogs and podcasts have been devoted to parents defending their decisions to allow children to use screens.

Parents excuse their screen usage in the name of getting things done or privacy:

'I can't cook dinner if my kids don't have a screen to look at.'

'I can't go to the toilet or have a shower in peace without a screen.'

And parents accuse others of excessive screen usage:

'You can't go to the park or to a restaurant without seeing parents ignoring their kids and staring at screens!'

Why the panic?

I used to believe that screens were neither good nor bad. Rather, it was what we did with them that was important. I am less convinced of this as time goes by. Each device and each app that is created for that device has been intentionally designed, often with input from hundreds or even thousands of engineers, psychologists, marketers and others, to be as compelling as possible. The people behind the devices and the apps are not neutral. They have a specific mission: to make people use their device or their app as much as possible.

It's ironic that for them to be successful, they need to make their devices and apps reduce *our* opportunities for success. As one simple example, some years ago Facebook realised that by making video play automatically, people would watch more and therefore remain on the platform longer. YouTube too created an autoplay system where new content automatically plays once the video you were watching is finished.

These design decisions didn't occur accidentally. Engineers, data-crunchers and design managers are consistently developing new ways of designing their products to keep us glued to the screen. As adults, we are often compelled to consume digital content, offering hours to scrolling through feeds and timelines. Our children are less capable of regulating their behaviour, and are at even greater risk of being consumed rather than being the consumer.

I believe that while the moral panic around screens may be over the top and sensationalised, the concerns about screens and digital media are well founded. I'll describe three things that concern me most before turning to the more important question: what do parents need to know to raise children who have a healthy balance with technology?

We'll consider three primary areas: wellbeing, physical health and brain development.

Wellbeing

Increasingly compelling data tells us that screens negatively impact wellbeing. Most of the data related to screens and wellbeing is based on studies of teenagers, primarily because (I assume) wellbeing is hard to measure in children under about eight or nine and they tend to access screens somewhat less than teens.

These are just a few brief study summaries to highlight the relationship between screen time and children's wellbeing.

- Two thousand Australian teens were studied from Year 8 until Year 11. Higher use of screens (for TV, Internet surfing, gaming or social media) in Years 8 and 9 increased the likelihood of depression, anxiety and other psychological difficulties in Years 10 and 11. *But* high levels of psychological distress did *not* predict problematic screen usage. The relationship only went one way; too much time on screens was what predicted lower wellbeing.

- The Monitoring the Future survey assesses adolescent wellbeing and gathers data on teen activities, including exercise, social interaction and screen time (such as social media and surfing the web). Results clearly indicate that teens who spend more time than average on screen activities are more likely to be unhappy, while those who are above average on time off-screen have significantly greater wellbeing. In fact, the more time spent on screens, the greater the reported level of depression.

- A group of young adults with Facebook pages received five texts per day for two weeks. Each time they received a text they reported their mood and the amount of time they'd been on Facebook. The more they used Facebook, the poorer their mood. (But those with poorer moods didn't use Facebook more.)

- Increased time on screens takes children away from interacting with their family and friends *in person*. As screen time goes up, so does agreement with statements like, 'A lot of times I feel lonely,' and, 'I often feel left out of things.'

What does this have to do with young children? You probably don't let your four-year-old use Facebook, so what's the big deal? A couple of things.

First, data indicates that even though children have to be 13 to be on Facebook, north of 90 per cent of children aged 8 to 12 are on it, and about 95 per cent of them signed up with their parents' help! We're crippling (or enabling) our children.

Second, kids are using screens more than ever. They may not be on social media, but they are on devices. Most important of all, studies show that screens interfere with relationships. Our kids are in the same home as we are, but they are talking with us less because of screens. Or are we talking to them less because of screens? Either way, this impacts wellbeing.

It's not just devices either. Studies in Australia, North America and Europe are consistently indicating that *television* is still a significant concern for children and young people's health. The official journal of the American Academy of Pediatrics highlights that as television and other screen viewing increased, so did children's later likelihood of depression, aggression and physical ill-health. (This was over and above any impact that low socio-economic background or education may have been responsible for.)

The best evidence from the American Academy of Pediatrics is clear. (And they devoted an entire supplementary section to their journal in late 2017 to highlight the following points.) Keep children away from screens as much as you can – for their own wellbeing. If they're under two, they shouldn't be getting *any* screen time. And once they are old enough for screens, we want to ensure it's a healthy digital diet. Not too much digital fairy floss and junk food. Sure, some mindless entertainment is fine here and there, just like some chocolate, chips and fizzy drink is a fun treat. But you don't give your children that kind of food for breakfast, lunch and dinner. You give them good, nutritional food – look for the equivalent in games, movies and television shows. Programs that focus on rescuing, exploring and relationships, or age-appropriate documentaries, are obviously healthier than those telling superhero stories, in which problems are solved using violence, for example.

Physical health

The healthier we are, the happier we are likely to be. Screens restrict and reduce movement. This affects mental and physical health. For children in kindergarten, more than one hour of screen time each day means they're 52 per cent more likely to be overweight than kids who watch less, and 72 per cent more likely to be obese than kids who watch less. The more they sit, the more they snack. In fact, children eat about 170 calories more per hour of TV watched than they would eat if they weren't watching TV.

Screens are given the blame for increasing eyesight problems in children. They get tired eyes and are at greater risk of needing glasses. Eye damage is a real and documented risk. The American Optometric Association suggests minimising screen time and sending children outside for the health of their eyes.

There seems to be some controversy over the extent to which screen time contributes to postural problems and head-and-neck injury. Some specialists I've spoken to suggest the idea is hype from the moral alarmists who don't want children looking at screens. Others argue that screens pose a serious structural risk to our children's necks, shoulders and spines.

But sleep is one area where there is no argument. Too many children are streaming instead of dreaming, connected to wifi and watching movies at the expense of sleeping. Increased exposure to screens means it takes *longer* to get to sleep, and it also means that sleep is of a *poorer* quality. Sleep is crucial for our brain to function well: during sleep it consolidates memories and is fortified for learning. The brain requires sleep so that it can remove waste products (from working all day), and process input and output. And we all know what lack of sleep does to our kids' moods.

HOW TO KNOW IF SOMEONE HAS A SCREEN-TIME PROBLEM

Think about how you, your partner or your child would score on the following questionnaire.

Answers should be given on a five-point scale: (0) Never, (1) Seldom, (2) Sometimes, (3) Often, (4) Very often	Score
1. How often do you find it hard to get off a screen once you're on one?	
2. How often do you stay on a screen even though you say you'll stop?	
3. How often do others (e.g. partner, children, parents, friends) say you should 'get off that screen now'?	
4. How often do you choose screen time over time with others?	
5. How often does screen time cost you sleep?	
6. How often do you find yourself wishing you were on a screen when you're not?	
7. How often do you think you should use screens less often?	
8. How often have you tried unsuccessfully tried to spend less time on screens?	
9. How often do you neglect the things you *should* be doing (work, school or family life) because you prefer to engage with your screens?	
10. How often do you use your screens as a distraction when you are feeling down?	
11. How often do you use a screen to escape or get relief from negative feelings?	
12. How often do you feel restless, frustrated or irritated when you cannot be on your screens?	

Total score: ___ out of 60

The higher the score, the more problematic screen usage may be for the person.

NOTE: Loosely adapted from the Compulsive Internet Use Scale (which is a questionnaire psychologists use to identify people who use the Internet and screens in compulsive and unhealthy ways). This scale will have limited applicability to young children but can be used as a helpful guide when considering whether screen time is becoming an issue.

Our children's brains

Brain-imaging studies are giving us incredible insight into what happens inside the heads of those who experience too much screen time. And if you think screens might be turning kids' brains to mush, you're not far wrong.

The first few years of life are considered a critical period – a time of extraordinary sensitivity – for brain development. This is a time when the brain's foundation is set, and upon which all later brain development and function is built. Our children's brains need important stimulation to develop healthily and naturally, and much of that comes from interacting with others as much as possible (especially parents), and using their bodies, including being outside climbing, running and exploring. Screens have a concerning impact on how our children's brains develop because they interrupt those crucial experiences during that critical phase of brain development. They provide endless stimulation for a child without them needing to move, go outside, explore or interact with anyone – all day in some cases!

Ironically, many parents give children tablets and screens to focus them, teach them and help them to develop, but the more screen time they get, the less effectively they function and grow. This is particularly important in the first few years of life, but continues to matter throughout childhood. The ability to focus, concentrate, pay attention, develop language and show empathy are all undermined with excessive screen time. (Conversely, reading literary fiction increases empathy.)

Story time traditionally meant a parent would read to a child as the child listened. Imagination was invigorated and relationships were strengthened. A picture on the page might be a starting point. And the child's brain would go into overdrive as she processed her mum's words to follow the story, imagining all of the things occurring as the plot tumbled from her mother's mouth. Devices reduce the cognitive load on a child. Devices do the thinking for them – or at least set boundaries around the thinking options they may have. Their brain can become lazy. Their cognitive muscles become soft and droopy.

Once they're older and compulsively using screens, brain scans show less brain volume in frequent screen users. Specifically, they have less grey matter (where information processing occurs). This means planning, prioritising, organising and controlling impulses all suffer. Damage to the insula, a portion of the cerebral cortex of the brain, has also been shown in problematic screen users, which is associated with a lack of empathy and compassion.

Brain scans also suggest that lots of screen time leads to slow, inefficient connections between brain cells. Communication in the brain can be compromised. And the brain's cortex is thinner among heavy screen users. They process information less efficiently and make poorer impulse-control decisions.

Kids who get a lot of screen time are shown to experience sensory overload. Everything is stimulating and it is exhausting. They have hyper-aroused nervous systems. They are less likely to function well in normal life and in relationships. And of course, they miss that restorative sleep so badly needed.

The way forwards

Reading all that – and acknowledging that we haven't touched on other areas, such as the social/relationship domain and the health of the spiritual/soul of the child – it is no wonder that there's a moral panic over screens!

But it's not all bad.

Appropriately balancing screen usage is a nuanced and challenging task. One child might spend hours on YouTube learning about astronomy and then tinkering with a telescope on the verandah in the evening, or learning about plants and growing things in the garden.

Other children may be consistently begging for more time on a screen so that they can play mindless games. This is worrisome. It is also natural since the programming is addictive and some of their parents are addicted themselves. Science, space and horticulture are entirely different from Disney, Spider-Man and the socialising and conditioning of pop culture.

But simply because some struggle, it doesn't mean we should penalise everyone, nor should we have a one-size-fits-all approach to rules. Getting the balance right is central to using screens well.

The unflinching fact is that screens are a part of our lives. We rely on devices for more and more functions. They are in every home, every educational context, every car (!!!) and everywhere else we go. Being alarmist and making screens a moral issue is unhelpful.

But we do need to know the risks so that we can identify a healthy and positive way forwards.

The latest guidelines from the American Academy of
Pediatrics (AAP) suggest that:

- children under 18 months should avoid screen time,
  other than video-chatting;

- children aged 18 months to two years can watch or use
  high-quality programs or apps if adults watch or play
  with them to help them understand what they're seeing;

- children aged two to five years should have no more than
  one hour a day of screen time with adults watching or
  playing with them;

- children aged six years and older should have consistent
  limits on the time they spend on electronic media and
  the types of media they use.

The following tips will help every parent guide their children to wise
choices regarding screens.

Be the example

We need to control technology rather than be controlled by it. We're
not doing so well. Neither are the children. Several studies conducted
over the past few years show that we – the parents – are the ones setting
the lousy example. In fact, our children hate it when they can't get to
us because we're glued to our screens. I have been guilty of telling my
children to get off their screens while I've been staring at mine. The
way we use our screens should mirror the way we consume food. Simply

because it's there on the table doesn't mean it must be eaten. We can say no to excessive food or the wrong kinds of food. And we can say no to excessive screen time or the wrong kinds of screen time.

We need rules – as do our children – when it comes to screen usage. The following key areas of content and context can guide the rules you choose to follow regarding screens in your home.

Watch the content

Content concerns are at the top of my list of worries regarding screens and children. Media reports, government inquiries and global conferences and summits have identified that the content children can access with the devices available at the dining table is simply *bad* for kids. Children as young as five are being expelled from schools as they enact or speak about explicit content that they have seen on screens now that every child who owns a device has porn in their pocket.

Our children are undeniably and unendingly exposed to content that is developmentally (and, in many cases, morally) inappropriate. Pornography and other explicit or exploitative content is at the top of the list. But violence and aggression, vulgarity and coarseness and adult themes (or teen themes being viewed by little ones) are increasingly viewed by children and young people, and evidence shows that exposure impacts both their beliefs and their behaviours.

If we move away from the explicit, coarse or violent content and just focus on children's programming, we still have some cause for concern. Much of children's television today is fast-paced, high-impact, aggressive or violent. Studies show that parents need to be discerning. This kind of content with non-stop bells and whistles and music and shouting may be having a significant negative impact on children's capacity to concentrate, their attention span and their cognitive and emotional development.

And then there's the even more subtle issues: most speaking roles are still being taken by male characters and we see ongoing marginalisation, tokenism and objectification of women in particular, but also those in minority races or religions.

The following questions can help you know whether the content your child is being exposed to is developmentally appropriate, or whether it may cause harm.

Are the characters in your child's screen viewing kind and positive?	Yes	No
Is there a genuinely educational element to this program or app?	Yes	No
Is the media your child is experiencing violent?	Yes	No
Is the media your child is experiencing scary?	Yes	No
Is the media your child is experiencing troubling?	Yes	No
Does the media your child is consuming encourage creativity or experimentation once the screen is off?	Yes	No
If you walked into a preschool or kindergarten and saw your child watching this program, would you feel that you were sending your child to a positive place?	Yes	No
Does the media encourage your child to communicate?	Yes	No
Is the content morally appropriate? (That is, nothing crude or explicit.)	Yes	No

Watch the context

There are times when screens are appropriate and there are times when they are universally not good at all. For example, if a child is under the age of two, most experts will agree that screens are unhelpful and should be avoided. (I prefer to recommend the age of three due to the sensitivity of the young brain to all that stimulation.)

Researchers have found – and emphasised heavily – that even having background television can be disruptive to a child's healthy development, interfering with speech and language development, cognitive development and social and emotional skills. Thriving children grow up in homes where screens are left off unless a specific program is being intentionally viewed.

When a child has friends visiting or is engaged in other activities that matter more, screens should be switched off. The dinner table, likewise, is a place where screens will typically do more harm than good, by stopping conversation, eye contact and interaction.

The following questions can help you know whether the context in which your child is watching screens is developmentally appropriate, or whether it may cause harm:

Is your child over the age of three?	Yes	No
Do you talk to your children about *why* screen rules are important?	Yes	No
Is the television switched off when not in use?	Yes	No
Do you highlight that even *you* have rules that you follow regarding screens because screens can be a problem for everyone?	Yes	No
Are screens switched off at least an hour before bedtime?	Yes	No
Do you have a special place for devices to be placed when friends visit, during meals or sleep time, or at other times when screen usage would be inappropriate?	Yes	No
Do you spend some time watching screens with your child so you are aware of content, but also so that you can be aware of your child as he engages with screens?	Yes	No
Do screens get switched off so conversations and social interaction can take place without interruption?	Yes	No
Are you discussing what your child is experiencing and exposed to while on screens?	Yes	No
Have you caught yourself missing out on cues from your child (or bids for connection) because of screens?	Yes	No
Do you regularly monitor both your children's program and screen access, including (where applicable) social interactions on their devices?	Yes	No
Do your children share family screens instead of each having devices of their own?	Yes	No

If you answered yes to most of these questions, you not only recognise the importance of being aware of the *content* your child consumes, but also the time and place it is being consumed. You're aware of what your child needs from you and even how the way you engage with screens affects your child. You keep screens out of bedrooms and encourage intentional use, where your child is in charge of the screen rather than the reverse.

Kids want time on screens? Walk them through this checklist to see whether it's good idea.

Have you:		
Played outside?	Yes	No
Spent time with a real person face to face?	Yes	No
Done your chores?	Yes	No
Read a book?	Yes	No
Done some exercise, gone for a walk or a ride, or been active some other way?	Yes	No
Helped someone in the family?	Yes	No
Tidied your room?	Yes	No
Prepared things for school tomorrow?	Yes	No
Had a chat with your grandparents on the phone?	Yes	No
Done something creative? (Art, music practice, etc?)	Yes	No
Finished any projects or other schoolwork?	Yes	No
Baked or cooked something?	Yes	No
Taken a bath?	Yes	No
Pursued a hobby?	Yes	No

Most parents would not demand that their child do everything on this list every day. It's not meant to be a checklist as much as a prompt for things your child might do instead of stare at a screen. By engaging in these activities, children will be experiencing a far more 'whole' childhood and doing more for their brain and body than a child who sits and stares at a screen.

Children will be more engaged in life, and screen time will be less interesting, when they do the things on this list – or other things like this.

There are many issues and challenges around screen usage for families. I have added questions to consider (with my suggestions for good answers) in the final chapter of the book, where you get to work together to determine your own family media plan.

Schools and device usage

Tech companies *want* our children to have devices, and they have cleverly convinced governments, education departments and many teachers that the earlier kids are computer literate, the better equipped they'll be to face the future. Many schools in Australia have embraced a 'Bring Your Own Device' style of program that, in some cases, begins in the first few years of school. Some schools mandate that every child must have a certain kind of device by Year 3. (I was told of one school that begins compulsory screen ownership in Year 1!)

However well intentioned, I believe such decisions lack sensitivity to family needs and income, parental priorities and children's development.

Bringing a device into the home creates a raft of challenges for many parents who prefer to minimise screen time and give their children access to and focus on other activities. Unwanted conflict often arises. Children may become deceptive at worst, and sedentary at best. Suddenly parents are dealing with screen challenges that otherwise would not have existed.

The best policies I have seen have come from thoughtful school leaders who have recognised this possible challenge and determined that, where devices are required in primary school years, they will only be used at school and will be kept at school overnight.

If you feel similarly, there is hope. One mum sought my advice.

> **The mum:** This year the school implemented a 1:1 iPad program and this has exponentially increased my Year 5 daughter's screen time (our house was screen-free Mon to Thurs and only minimal screen time on the weekend) as well as increasing her homework burden. The problem is that homework has changed from being practice of sums or spelling, for example, to doing research online or completing tasks in preparation for classes. This limits my ability to put my foot down and tell her teacher that she will not be completing homework as it then impacts on her ability to keep up at school. I would love to hear any advice you have. Many thanks. K.

> **Me:** Let the teacher know your thoughts. See if there's any wiggle room or a strong reason why screens are a must. Perhaps homework might be done on paper (or better yet, reduced or eliminated).

> **The mum:** Hi Dr Justin, thought you might be interested in an update. My husband met with our daughter's teacher to inform

her she would no longer be completing iPad-based homework, given she is having usually over one hour and up to two hours on it at school. She was very supportive of our wish to keep the house a sanctuary from the iPad and seemed to really like the idea. She also said that she had noticed a difference in our daughter of late in that she is usually quite energised and motivated but it was taking her longer to get up and into things at school. She has agreed to support us by providing all homework in paper format but did say that our daughter may be required on occasion to complete group-based project work on the iPad in preparation for class time. I am comfortable with this. If it is too often, we will tell her she will not be completing those tasks either. Our daughter is happy and has returned to playing with dolls, Lego and baking. I think it will take a bit of time but I see her starting to relax again. In addition to this, we have reinstated our no screen time after school rule. If it is to be broken, it is strictly half an hour and only TV, not iPad time. I am pleased with the outcome. I feel like I have my daughter back and am seeing positive results. Thanks for your advice.

There's also the question of tech and making sure that our children don't miss out on opportunities to become competent coders. Exposure to screens, many suggest, is what kids need so that they can become familiar with the technology age and not get left behind. In his book *Deep Work*, computer scientist Cal Newport states in response to this argument:

The complex reality of the technologies that real companies leverage to get ahead emphasises the absurdity of the now common idea that exposure to simplistic, consumer-facing products – especially in schools – somehow prepares people to succeed in the high-tech economy. Giving students iPads or allowing them to film homework assignments on YouTube prepares them for a high-tech economy about as much as playing with Hot Wheels would prepare them to thrive as auto-mechanics.

The argument is without foundation, and is unlikely to do anything for our children except give them more opportunities to get lost in entertainment (in all its varieties) and much that is mindless and distracting from living a whole and balanced life.

Take-home message

If we were going to give advice based purely on evidence, it would be this: put away the screens, stow the phone and do something – do *anything* – that does not involve screens.

Our children don't need smartphones. They need smart parents. Just because everyone else has an iPad or a telephone does not mean your child requires one.

The moral panic around screens may be a little OTT from time to time, but it is well founded. Screens are impacting wellbeing, relationships, physical health and academic learning. There has been a measurable decrease in our children's psychological health that spiked shortly after 'smart' devices appeared on the market. It is up to us to give our children a wide range of experiences that will develop them as a *whole* child. Screens will inevitably be a part of their world, but they will ideally only be a small part.

8

Protecting childhood

Indulge me in being far too predictable as we begin this chapter. I'm going straight in to *nostalgia*. Nostalgia is a sad feeling about a past that cannot be reclaimed.

I was born in the 1970s. (It seems like that was a long time ago, but I don't feel that old!) My parents raised me in a lower-to-middle-class suburb. Mum and Dad ran their own business and worked long hours. I walked home from school, let myself in and was free to play anywhere in the neighbourhood until they returned from work each afternoon.

My weekday afternoons were spent riding my bike with my best mate, Andy. We would hang out in the local park until dark. We visited school friends. We sat around in one another's living rooms, raided our parents' fridges and pinched spare change from the kitchen bench to fritter away on junk food or arcade games at the nearby shop. We played marbles. We kicked the footy. We climbed trees. Does that sound as idyllic to you as it does me?

I did all of this from around the age of seven or eight. If you're even close to my age, you probably enjoyed similar freedoms and opportunities.

I want the same for my children, but it is increasingly unusual and increasingly unobtainable for many. Questions about safety abound.

Children have ever-increasing academic loads. Schedules for both children and their parents are busier than ever. Extra-curricular activities are more popular than ever. Screens have proliferated. And downtime is harder to find than ever before.

What has happened to our children's childhoods?

This chapter is about protecting childhood and letting kids be kids. I'm going to emphasise four central themes. First, the need for play: developmentally appropriate and (eventually) unsupervised play. Second, the importance of letting go of the pressure around schooling. The increased hand-wringing associated with school starting age, homework and how well our children do on their tests is harming kids. Third, the imperative to reduce competition, comparison and the push to 'be more and do more'. And fourth, the possibility that our children can be calm.

The need for play

Play is integral to building successful, resilient children. And it matters from the earliest ages. When they are young, infants need parents to play with them through touch, making sounds, peek-a-boo and by lying on the floor beside them and engaging however the baby wants. Sing-song talk, lots of face-to-face and eye-to-eye communication and playful interaction (so long as the baby isn't sleepy or irritable).

Toddlers enjoy activities and tactile play. They want to pull things apart to see how they work. (This can be frustrating and expensive.) They struggle to understand why the DVD player will work with a DVD but not Vegemite toast. As they become close to age three or four, they start to enjoy some social time, too. Dress-ups and role-playing characters become exciting. Their brains are developing and they are starting to explore social and emotional worlds. At this age, you're still their number one playmate though.

Preschoolers want to make a mess! Water play, sand play, mud play. It's all fun. Play dough, macaroni and feathers with some craft paper and glue – anything that allows their artistic creativity to come out will light them up.

At preschool age our children start to want to climb, run, explore and be active in their play. Trampolines are an endless source of joy. So are big cardboard boxes. And more dress-ups. Because their language is improving, silly songs and rhymes become fun – and yes, their tolerance for repetition remains strong. The more, the better! They love sorting and counting – threading and stacking. Playtime with friends will work for most children, but frustrations will occur around sharing or tiredness. You're *still* their number one. And they love to be involved with cooking, stirring and washing up. (Be warned, it gets messy.)

Once your children are in early primary school they'll still enjoy childish play. Craft, art, messing around in water and building dams or sandcastles. They'll still love an indoor cubby in the lounge room or a big box to hide in or 'drive' around the house in. But by around Years 2 or 3, games with rules will become important. Social interaction will be a central focus. They need friends to play with. They'll be increasingly interested in being outdoors riding a bike or playing sport. With their ever-developing language skills, thinking skills (for understanding rules) and physical coordination, being active is usually fun. The more unstructured play our children can have before the age of about ten, the better for them.

When children are allowed to play, they develop important skills. They establish boundaries and learn to understand other people. Social norms are transmitted through play. They learn to negotiate and share, stick up for themselves and make decisions. Play, at any age, helps children learn to manipulate or interact with their environment and with others. They learn to be creative explorers. A stick becomes a magic wand or sword or a spoon for stirring a magic pudding.

Maybe the most fun play available for children under ten is rough-and-tumble wrestling play with a parent. During this kind of play, children learn about limits. They communicate. They are physical. And they laugh.

A mum in one of my seminars shared a story:

> My youngest is now 23 and all of my children have moved out of home. On the weekend, we had all the kids around for a BBQ. They started talking about favourite family memories. One of the boys mentioned wrestles with Dad. Everyone agreed that was the most fun, and my youngest reminded us all of the time I joined in. He looked at me and told me, 'Mum, I think that might be my most fun memory of you ever.'

My experience suggests that we need to be careful when mums get involved though. Someone always ends up crying! Don't get too rough, Mum!

Regardless of how you play, the best things about all of these suggestions is that they're easy, they're healthy, they're mostly educational (in fact they lead to optimal outcomes) and they're low-cost or no-cost!

Play really is the work of childhood, and it establishes a foundation on which resilient lives rest.

Extra tips for playing with infants and toddlers

1. **Let your child take the lead.** Give your child something – anything really – to explore and play with. Watch what they do. Give them maximum autonomy. The more we try to show them the 'right' way to use it, the less motivated they will be. Studies show that, long-term, kids who are too controlled have less intrinsic motivation and may even exhibit less resilience.

2. **Go slow.** Whether you are reading or playing, 'slow' is the key word. You might show a child some ways that something could be used. But then step back. Let them creatively explore. Watch their curiosity develop.

3. **Be responsive.** If you see frustration creeping in, you might help them a little. Or perhaps you might simply offer some encouragement. Be aware of whether your child is too tired or hungry for play. You can tell when they are bored with a game or just tired.

4. **Minimise distractions**.

5. **Provide variety.** If your child loves water play, try some slime or some sand. If your child loves painting, try crayons or some other texture.

6. **Repeat.** And repeat. And repeat. (Should I say it again?) And repeat. It will probably drive you crazy, but repetition is how your child learns. They can tolerate something at least 200 times more than you or I can! Yup, peek-a-boo really is still funny after the 400th 'boo'! The more they practise, the more mastery they experience. Competence and mastery are so vitally important for our children, and as they develop, they seek more.

―――――――――――――――

School readiness

Finland is one of the world's leading countries in education. Their children are among the most numerate and literate in the world, consistently at the top of the table in international comparisons. Their approach to learning in the first years of school? Play!

Not maths. Not reading and writing. No special tests before school starts to see how advanced or disadvantaged the kids might be. They get all of the children together to ... play. In fact, in Finland, learning during the first years of school is not about getting the spelling words right and doing well on tests. It's about *joy, exploration* and *creativity*.

Why?

When children feel good, they learn well. When they feel bad, they rarely learn at all. An old Finnish saying teaches, 'Those things you learn without joy, you will forget easily.'

This is a lesson that appears to have been forgotten by Australian educators – or perhaps by policy makers. In the interests of economic growth and ensuring our children don't get 'left behind' educationally, there is a never-ending push to send children to school earlier and a corresponding expectation that younger children will be capable of reaching higher educational standards earlier than ever before.

These decisions are unwise and developmentally inappropriate.

Australian researchers Amanda Mergler and Sue Walker found that parents are experiencing anxiety over the simple decision about when to send their children to school. As different agendas of politicians and educators clash with the economic realities and the specific needs of families (and the well-meaning advice of other parents), people feel stuck. Is he ready for school? What does *ready for school* look like?

The more I study this topic, the more convinced I am that children are advantaged when formal schooling is delayed until as late as seven. There is obviously a *big* gap between the early start of age four, and the later age of seven. The most successful countries in education in the world use this approach, but they also provide lots of stimulating play environments for those four-, five- and six-year-old children. In addition to the success they have in supporting later formal schooling, two other key statistics tell me that something is wrong with the push for more and more, earlier and earlier:

1. **The number of children in prep/kindergarten getting expelled from school is at record levels**. While the numbers aren't extraordinarily high, they're going up fast. Over 1000 children aged four or five were expelled from Queensland schools in 2016. (Essentially double the previous year's figures.)

2. **Research is telling us that the youngest children in a class are more likely than their older classmates to receive medication for ADHD** (Attention Deficit Hyperactivity Disorder). The data suggest – not for the first time – that children are being misdiagnosed with ADHD. We're potentially medicating age-related immaturity! And no, it's not just that kids with ADHD are being sent to school early because parents need a break! When the researchers looked at the data, they found that among the children aged six to ten, those born in June – the last month of a recommended school year intake – were about twice as likely to have received ADHD medication than those born the previous July. For children aged 11 to 15, the effect was less marked 'but still significant'. And when they extended the question to a comparison of those born in the first three (or six) months and the last three (or six) months of the school year intake, the effect remained. (Obviously each state

has a different cut-off date for school commencement,
but that data should hold regardless of which month we
assess. Younger children are at increased risk.)

Frankly, I find this astounding and appalling. And parents need to be equipped to make informed decisions to help their children thrive rather than merely survive.

What is going on here? I believe we are robbing our children of the chance to be kids. We need to let them be little, but instead we are applying too much pressure and expectation too soon.

When we try to get children to learn things earlier, we often are fighting the realities of development. It is best to teach any subject to children when their minds are ready. When we rush the process, children get frustrated and may learn to hate education.

Children used to start school at around age five, and their first year was essentially play-based learning. Now they are encouraged to start earlier. There are (in most states) 'tests' that aren't really tests, where students are assessed for their ability to read and write, among other things, *before they've even started school.*

I asked one teacher why this 'assessment' was happening and she told me, 'Oh, it's just so we can see where they're up to and to help us fill in any gaps.'

> **Me:** Gaps? She's four years old! Everything is a gap! That's why we send them to school.

Combined with the additional pressure around 'school readiness', children are *still* expected to do homework in those early years, despite zero evidence to support its usefulness. Data are clear that reading is great for kids' learning and school success, but in primary school, homework has a neutral impact on learning and achievement *at best*. And it all too often has a negative effect.

The letter I send to school each year about homework
Homework is a hot-button issue in families and classrooms around the world. Most parents not only assume that homework will be part of their child's education, they demand it.

But let's face it. Most kids hate it. They would almost all prefer to do something – anything – other than homework. You'll be hard-pressed to find parents who enjoy it (though most endorse it), and there are few teachers who are fond of the extra work associated with homework. Plus, research shows it's unhelpful for children in primary school.

In fact, many primary schools are rethinking homework entirely, with some principals banning it altogether. And yes, I've actually banned my children from doing homework before high school.

So I have written a letter to teachers – for you. It's about why your kids don't need to do homework.

Dear Teacher,

We are delighted to have our child in your classroom. She seems to be extremely happy with her class and is thrilled to have you as her teacher. Our child is a diligent and conscientious student with an amazing attitude. We trust that you are enjoying having her in your class, and she is making a great contribution.

We are writing to share with you a (hopefully minor) conflict our family has with school policy. The issue is homework. Barring two exceptions, which we'll mention in a moment, we do not encourage homework in our home. The reasons for this are as follows:

1. **Scientific**. For young children (under around age 14 years) there is no scientific research which supports the inclusion of homework in their after-school activities. Even the Victorian Government's Senate Inquiry into homework failed to find solid support for the practice.

2. **Practical**. Homework may add to your workload. We know how hard you work already. Homework just gives you more to do on top of an already huge task load.

3. **Stress**. Homework creates stress for our children. Research has demonstrated that homework overwhelms struggling kids and removes joy for high achievers. Some researchers have found a direct relationship between time spent on homework and levels of anxiety, depression, anger and other mood disorders and issues. I want my kids to be happy and balanced, not depressed and anxious.

4. **Burdens**. Homework creates an extra burden on us as parents. With six children, a business, and myriad other priorities, this is one thing we believe is dispensable. Plus, once they hit Year 4, we don't know how to do what the kids are being asked!

5. **Conflict**. Homework creates family conflict.

6. **Balance**. Homework diminishes the time our children have for other activities that supplement schooling and learning.

    We have our children involved in music lessons, sports, church activities and more. Additionally, the children enjoy being children, by swimming in the pool, playing with friends, having free reading time, going shopping, contributing in our home with chores and cooking and so on.

7. **Character**. Does it really grow character? There is no evidence to support the belief that homework helps students develop the characteristics it is often recommended as promoting, such as ability to organise time, develop good work habits, think independently and so on. It doesn't seem to prepare them for 'later' either. They can usually adapt pretty well when they turn 14 or 15 without having eight years of practice under their belt before it all starts.

Our position on homework can essentially be summarised by a quote from US literacy expert Harvey Daniels: 'Most of what homework is doing is driving kids away from learning.'

We mentioned two exceptions to our homework rule:

1. **Reading**. Our children read every day before bed. But we don't say that they have to do it for X minutes or they stare at the clock, and we don't say X pages or they'll find the easiest books with the fewest words. As a result, we often get them in trouble for reading too much!

   We have seen that the best way to make students hate reading is to make them prove to us or others that they have read. On a related note, we discourage the use of rewards for behaviour – such as stars, goodies, etc. However, we DO let the children know that when they have completed a book we will gladly buy them another one immediately, or take them to the library for more if budget is an issue. This, we find, is highly motivating.

2. Projects. Our other form of 'acceptable' homework is
related to projects from school that interest the
children. We actively encourage research projects
and especially writing speeches and stories. This
helps the children in information gathering, critical
thinking, logical formatting of content and presentation
skills. Plus, it gets them actively 'discovering' in their
learning, and sinks in much deeper than much other
'busy' work.

We do not want to undermine you or make your
job more difficult. In fact, we believe that it will
make things easier for everyone and assist in the
well-rounded positive developmental outcomes for
our children.

Thanks so much for reading this. We hope that you
can be understanding of our position and are happy to
discuss this with you if you have any concerns.

Now, a confession.

First, my position on homework has softened marginally since I
first wrote this letter in 2007. Why? Well, I've seen some kids who were
struggling at school and who, with patient help from parents or tutors,
have been helped to excel (or at least catch up) by homework.

Second, some kids just love doing homework. I'm not about to
suggest that they should be forced to stop.

Third, a careful look at the research shows that while homework
makes no difference – and can be negative – for the average child, your
child may not be average. This means that in some cases, homework
may be helpful. I say this tentatively though, because any differences are
likely to be small and they can often come at great cost.

If your children are in primary school and want to do homework, that's up to you. If they don't, it would seem they don't need it. If your kids are struggling, talk with your teacher. Consider your individual circumstances and listen to your child.

Standardised testing

In the past decade we have added a $100 million standardised test named NAPLAN for children as young as eight, adding more pressure to already over-examined, over-drilled students in the name of transparency and accountability for teachers, and higher achievement for our children. But the data, not just in Australia but worldwide, indicate that these tests are devastating for academic achievement, and extinguish children's interest in learning.

I have written extensively about NAPLAN's negatives elsewhere and you'll find a critique of the test in the back of the book. For now, the key point is this: evidence shows children feel increased anxiety and pressure. There is an associated downwards push on academic expectations that children in the earliest years of school feel.

The pressures of NAPLAN and homework combine with earlier-aged starts, and the expectation that rather than playing, they'll sit at a desk all day and listen. Movement is reduced. Play is less common now than ever. And four-year-olds, in particular, often cannot cope.

This reminds us of the challenging fact that more and more children are being expelled from school at this tender age, and that more and more of them are being medicated – even the youngest ones.

There is no doubt that some of these children will be experiencing mental health issues, family problems, economic difficulties and more. But when we say that all six-year-olds should be able to sit still and learn, or that all Year 3 children should be able to do x or y, we're ignoring developmental differences that are normal. The reality is that not all children can do these things at these ages. We don't demand that our second child walk at ten months just because her older sibling could! We must be sensitive to different developmental paths in children.

Data also tell us that the number of young children (under the age of eight) who are now medicated for depression, anxiety or stress is at an all-time high. It is amazing to me that we are medicating such young children to the level that statistics suggest. We are raising the *most medicated* generation in the history of the world.

We need to give our children *skills*, not *pills*. And they don't get those skills from sitting in a classroom all day from the age of four, facing desks, and learning passively. They get skills from playing – without adults – and experiencing life with their peers. From exploring and creating and doing those things described at the start of the chapter. Their bodies need to be used to develop healthily.

These numbers are disappointing, but not surprising. Suspensions, expulsions and medications are surely related to the push for formal learning from the age of four, and the diminished access to play. Challenges with behaviour are complex and may be related to any number of issues, but I am convinced that these first years of school should be about enjoying school like preschoolers used to: in a fun, exciting, creative play-based setting. This is where they learn to share, follow rules, take turns, communicate, problem-solve, develop empathy, to regulate their own behaviour and to become resilient. Along the way they'll incidentally learn some writing and number skills as well. But when we remove play, we remove the opportunities for them to learn and practise these things.

School readiness has come to mean 'Can this child sit for long periods, and read and write?' This is an unwise and inappropriate standard, but unfortunately means we then claim that our children aren't meeting the standard, and then we push them harder – or in some extremely problematic cases, we punish them. We hurt them rather than help them.

For those struggling children, a bad experience like this may disengage them, turning them off school and learning for a lifetime. They may come to hate education – and even life.

We must slow down and stop rushing. Studies show that in the long run, children who learn to read or write earlier aren't any better off in reading than those who lag. A study by New Zealand's Dr Sebastian Suggate found that teaching a child to read from age five is not likely to make that child any more successful at reading than one who learns reading later, from age seven. Comparing children from Rudolf Steiner schools, who usually start learning to read from age seven, and children in state-run schools, who start learning to read at five, Suggate found that the later learners caught up and matched the reading abilities of their earlier-reading counterparts by the time they were 11, or by Year 7.

Perhaps we can let them be little. While not all children are failing, too many are struggling, and those who struggle the most are typically our most vulnerable children.

We protect our children's chance to be children and extend their childhood by allowing them to start school a little later and with less pressure. We let them be little longer by reducing the unnecessary and counter-productive burden of homework and refusing to push them into meaningless and competitive standardised testing. Instead, we encourage play-based learning, exploration and creativity, and time with friends. These are the things that protect childhood and build a resilient future for our children.

Lastly, there is a shift in direction within schools. Some now argue that to prepare children for the future, where robots will do all of the work, STEM skills will be important. The tech-driven future demands the shift. Others argue strongly for bringing psychology to the classroom because the ability to develop empathetic/relational skills will be the answer – again because of our increasingly tech-driven future. The truth is that nobody knows what the world will be like 20 years from now. I suspect it will be very different from today. Given this uncertainty in a fast-changing world, I think the most important things to learn in school are 'learning to learn'. By making the decisions around homework and NAPLAN I've highlighted here, I believe we can encourage greater motivation to learn for learning's sake, which will be good for all of us.

Protecting Childhood was formed in response to the current trend to push formal academic direct instruction down into the early years of school and preschools without regard for the developmental needs and readiness of children. I'm an ambassador for Protecting Childhood, and I asked them to share their goals and their tips for helping kids be kids.

Protecting Childhood's goals are to:

- educate and inform parents on 'normal' child developmental expectations and readiness;

- counter the fear-based rhetoric of politicians and media that we're 'falling behind';

- inspire and encourage teachers and principals to reinvent schools as learning communities who are dedicated to wellbeing, emotional and social literacy and developing the skills (collaboration, communication, creativity and critical thinking) and the lifelong learning dispositions needed to navigate a future we cannot predict; and

- empower parents and teachers to advocate for the children in their care, to have their needs prioritised over the needs of the system.

They argue that these five tenets can help protect childhood.

1. **Readiness is a broad continuum**. Listen to your heart. If you're unsure if your four- or five-year-old is 'ready' for formal school, you can delay entry (check with your state education department for ages) and/or seek out a school with a play-based pre-primary philosophy. If your five-year-old is not interested in reading yet, know that they are not 'behind'. Learning to love reading is more important than learning to read.

2. Withdraw your child from high-stakes standardised testing (e.g. NAPLAN) and the preceding 'preparation' for it. Each year I withdraw my children from this expensive, corporate-driven test. Tell the government that you **value learning over testing and ranking**.

3. Consider **alternative learning environments**, where physiological and psychological needs come first, especially if your child is coming home angry, teary or anxious, or is refusing and avoiding school regularly.

4. **Don't battle over homework**. Homework is counter-productive if it makes home a place of tensions and has been shown to have little or zero benefit in primary school. (Reading is important, however, so always read to your children and encourage them to read themselves when appropriate.)

5. Ensure your schedule has **unstructured, child-led play** (screen-free). Creativity is born from boredom. **Spend time in nature** and let children take healthy physical risks.

Doing too much?

Helping our children enjoy childhood is not just about reducing the pressure around schooling. There's the question of extra-curricular activities. Sport and other pursuits are increasingly common at younger ages. Countless blog articles and even books have been written about whether our children are overscheduled. Experts and parents fear that kids are doing too much. They dramatically stir up concern that parents' expectations are too high. Alarmists are screaming that the sky is falling and children are being deprived of a childhood because they have too many adults telling them what to do and when to do it, and how they could have done it better.

Raising talented children (or at least raising children who have opportunities to develop talents) has become a competitive sport among some parents too, trying to outdo others with the impressive accomplishments of their child.

So do we need to ease off on the throttle? Or should we be exposing our children to as much enrichment as they can take? (And yes, budget has got to play a part. Some people reading this are wishing they could afford to have this problem.)

At the outset, let's acknowledge that free play and unstructured time is important for our children's wellbeing. That's been well established throughout this chapter, but it bears repeating in relation to extra-curricular activity. Kids need free time. They need the opportunity to play, explore, be curious and creative, and be still. The more we schedule activities for them, the less free time, downtime and free play they have time for.

For many of us, however, it just works to get the children involved in (carefully chosen) extra-curricular experiences. This is particularly the case when children are younger. Why?

First, we're no longer living in the 1950s. Parents are working outside the home, the streets aren't nearly as child-friendly as they were and expectations around what's safe for children have shifted. When our kids are in some form of structured activity, they're safe and they're developing. That's two big boxes we've just ticked! We're making their lives better by ensuring they can play the guitar or dance or swim. While it costs money, we feel reassured that they're in good hands *and* they're not wasting their lives doing nothing … or worse, staring at that screen.

Second, with the screen tsunami that has swept society, any opportunity our children may have for some 'down' time or free play is all-too-often subsumed by those screens. The benefits we seek are easily trumped by the digital distractions that are ever-present.

Third, we are maximising! We feel good knowing we're helping our children become all that they can be.

Fourth, when I leave my children alone for that 'free-range' style of play, there's a chance that someone ends up hurting a sibling. They fight.

Finally (and at the risk of being a bit too honest), when the children have an activity to participate in, we don't need to make any decisions or deal with any issues around childcare, bored children and keeping them occupied ourselves. It's all outsourced and made easy. Yes, there's the inconvenience of getting them there and home, but the learning and development – and the 'care' – are done by others. While most parents aren't doing this to make life easier, there are times when it definitely does – and that can be a GOOD thing! We all appreciate a bit of down-time where the kids are taken care of in positive activities and we don't have to think about it.

From a practical and psychological perspective, having the children involved in extra-curricular activities is the answer. No screens. No fighting. Learning. Safe. Optimised.

Research also tells us there are other benefits to structured activities. Sports give the opportunity for social skills, academic improvement,

physical health, psychological wellbeing and more. Music and the arts improve children's memory, academic capacity, social skills and so on. All of these activities potentially enhance feelings of competence, build relationships and promote wellbeing.

With all of these benefits, it makes sense to do even more of this, doesn't it? Shouldn't we embrace the benefits and push harder for more opportunity? Or is there a reason experts are clamouring to remind us that it's all too much, that we should pull back from extra-curricular opportunities and give our children more space to be children with no commitments or pressures or growth demands.

There is a line that balances the competing demands of structure, growth and enrichment with stress, financial costs and protecting childhood. The problem is none of us really knows where that line is until we've crossed it. And it's different for each child ... and it changes as they mature and develop.

Rather than me telling you where to draw that line, here are some questions to ask yourself to get the balance right for your children.

Am I anxious about my child's success in life, or am I trying to improve my child's wellbeing?

In other words, am I doing this because I want my kids to get ahead? Or am I doing this because it enhances their quality of life? The answer could be 'both', but this potentially means that it's about success and your anxiety about whether they'll be good enough. 'I'm doing this for you' can be said with sincerity, but it can also be said to mask the possibility that we are really doing this for ourselves and *our* view of what we think our child needs, regardless of their feelings. Look deep inside and listen closely to understand your motivations.

Does your child feel like you care about the outcomes more than they do?

If your child gets the sense that missing that goal on the soccer field, not being selected for the rep team or not placing in the eisteddfod means they're not good enough, then you may want to rethink participation in the activity. This is meant to be about them having fun and learning. It's not about them being the best and beating the best. When performance becomes a way of demonstrating personal worth and determining self-esteem, we've missed the point. If we care more about it than they do, we *may* have stepped over the line.

Sometimes we care more about the outcomes because we care more about them and their lives than they do. We really do believe that if they are a concert pianist or a representative soccer player or {insert excellence in specific activity here} that their lives will be better. Sometimes we may be right. But plenty of people can't play an instrument and are still, surprisingly, wonderful, happy, productive humans.

Sometimes our children are simply unmotivated. This is unfortunate when we know we are giving them an opportunity for enrichment that is genuinely valuable. But generally speaking, if they don't care and you do, you may have pushed things further than is worthwhile.

This doesn't mean we should simply let them quit, by the way. In some cases, we might suggest that they're 'so close' to the point of enjoying and mastering the activity that a little more persistence will be worth it. Our wisdom may be persuasive in these instances. Perhaps your child has signed up to play for a team, so finishing the season is a commitment that should usually be kept.

Are your kids excited to participate?

When you take your child to their lessons or sports, are they laughing, smiling and energised? Or are they complaining and dragging their feet? Their energy levels around this activity can be a useful indicator of whether it's working or not. There will be times when what they are doing is hard. They will lose motivation if they can't master something. Persistence is sometimes required. But you will know they want to be there by the degree to which you convince, cajole and coerce your child to get involved.

There are some practical things to consider that may influence your decision as well.

Does your child have time to play with friends?

Are they getting enough sleep?

Does your child get free play time?

Do you make time to do nothing alone, and together?

The research tells us that our children benefit greatly from structured, planned, formal activities. If we have the resources, these activities are great for our children's development. But age may be a factor.

Before about age ten, participation in structured activities should be limited and *all* about fun. If they want to play sport or be involved in music and drama, this should be encouraged. But participation should be self-determined rather than directed by us. And the purpose is nothing but fun and mastery. Scores are irrelevant. Best and fairest awards are redundant. Competitiveness, exams and progression are secondary to enjoyment, mastery and relationships.

The entire focus should be letting children be children.

Once the kids get to ten, let them choose. Give them options. Enrich their lives. It doesn't matter so much how many activities they're doing at this age. What matters is the messages you send about their participation in those activities, and the extent to which they enjoy them.

The questions on the previous page can help you get the balance right.

Even more important is the message they receive from you about how important they are to you. And that doesn't come from time in activities. It comes from time with you.

As with schooling, it is not about competition, comparison and being enough. It's not a race. It's not about who gets there first. It is a time for exploration, learning and creativity. US education expert Alfie Kohn states that:

> When we set children against one another in contests – from spelling bees to awards assemblies to science 'fairs' (that are really contests), from dodge ball to honour rolls to prizes for the best painting or the most books read – we teach them to confuse excellence with winning, as if the only way to do something well is to outdo others. We encourage them to measure their own value in terms of how many people they've beaten ... Finally, we lead children to regard whatever they're doing as a means to an end ... The act of painting, reading or designing is thereby devalued in the child's mind.

We want our children to love learning, love life, love people and love opportunities to solve problems. We don't want them to merely beat others in artificial contests.

Take-home message

Childhood is shrinking. Those years of carefree innocence are being crowded out with education agendas, personal development plans and fewer opportunities for play and exploration. As play has declined, kids have become more anxious and depressed. They lose control over their lives as we take over, dictate, drive and demand. Yet play, curiosity, slow and agenda-free development and the chance to pursue interests that align with personal strengths are some of the most important gifts we can give a child to truly experience *childhood*. They get to make their own decisions, write their own rules and have their own experiences. There's a strong connection with feeling in control of our lives and being happy. When our children see us, they do not need to be burdened with more work and study. They need us to fall on the floor, tickle, wrestle and laugh. They need opportunities to learn and create; to sit quietly on the grass under a tree and stare at clouds; to experience the simplicity of childhood; and to simply be. As we give them back their childhood, they won't seem to be so old so young.

9

Feeling joy

My friend Rob was a devoted father of three children in their teens. Rob was a gentle man. He never seemed rattled or perturbed. Instead, he was calm about everything. He never seemed in a rush. He took time to talk and, more importantly, to listen. Rob was not wealthy, but he was content.

Rob loved to sing, especially with his children. And Rob loved to play games. Whenever I visited Rob, he was in the living room or at the dining table playing games or singing. And at least one of the children was always there with him. In fact, Rob used to intentionally sit in the living room and do nothing. It's not that he was lazy. Rob knew that if he sat in the lounge chair without an agenda, with nothing to do, his children would wander by, stop, sit with him and talk. Rob knew what joy in family life was, and his wife and children experienced it with him.

As I wrote this book, Rob's heart stopped beating. He passed away, just shy of 50.

Thoughts coursed through my mind over the ensuing days. I grieved the loss of a friend. I grieved for Rob's wife, now widowed and in mourning. And I grieved for those three children who had lost a deeply loved father. I was reminded of my own mortality. I contemplated that Rob didn't know that his last hug with his wife and each of his children would be that night. Nor did they. None of them knew that his quick glance and cheeky smile would be the last living moment with their dad; that the gentle brush of his hand across their shoulder would be their last living touch of the man they loved so dearly.

Rob reminded me of some lessons that I teach often. Rob made sure he was available to his family. He put away tasks that would interfere with conversation and made himself present. He invited games and fun. He smiled and told stories. He laughed and sang songs.

He didn't disappear for games of golf on Saturday or for long brunches in a café. 'Me-time' didn't matter to him. It was all about 'we-time'. His family was everything to him. He loved them. Most importantly, they knew it.

We don't all have the capacity to sit in the living room for long periods of time. We all have commitments and obligations. We all have livings to earn, hobbies and pastimes, a desire to improve our health or finish a book. We have meals to cook, rooms to clean and lives to live. Rob did too. But he minimised them so he could focus on what mattered most. And his family was the richer for it.

An old poem by Erma Bombeck, titled 'If I had my life to live over', reminds us of the things that really bring us joy – the things that matter most. Those things include talking less and listening more, building friendships and having people in our home even if it's messy, lying on the lawn with the kids without worrying about grass stains, laughing and crying less at the television but more at life. Most important, she says she would not have brushed away those hugs and kisses from children expressing love, and she would have said 'I love you' and 'I'm sorry' more.

Watching Rob's family in the months following his passing prompted me to ask some questions that I see as valuable for all families. What would you do differently in your family if you knew that you had one month or one week or one day left? How would you express your love differently? How would you experience joy?

Children don't make us happy ...
or do they?

Our children need to feel joy in our homes and in their relationships with us. Too often, we cram so much into our lives (and theirs) that this becomes a challenge. We're too busy. They're too busy. We don't sit in the living room (with the screens off) and enjoy being together. We get cranky. We punish rather than teach. We don't stop or look or listen. We stare at screens because it's the path of least resistance. And some days, we raise the white flag, say it's all too hard and become either victims of the challenges of family life or grumpy stressheads.

There are times that it feels completely appropriate to be a grump and banish joy. We've all had to pick up poo out of the bath with our bare hands or clean marker pen off walls; we've all woken up to vomit-stained carpet in the kids' room. Most of us have experienced a strong-willed child. And nearly all of us are sleep-deprived. Yes, it is hard. Very hard. But no matter what it is that is making us unhappy, dwelling on it and ruminating about it is guaranteed to make things worse!

Learning that children create unhappiness in our lives was perhaps the most surprising discovery of my psychology studies. It was my unhappiness in parenting that drove me to spend close to a decade studying the topic, sure, but I had assumed I was an anomaly. I was the weird one. Everyone else had it together, or so I thought. To discover that ALL of the evidence highlights that parental happiness drops when the first child is born and decreases until the last-born leaves the nest was a fearful revelation for me. 'Do you mean, kids make us unhappy? All of us?'

I discussed this with many parents – and still do – and the response was always the same. 'Nope. Not true for me. I love my children. They make me happy.'

This perplexed me. Do children bring us joy or misery? The research says they make us miserable. The mum blogs and Facebook feeds reinforce this idea. But everyday mums and dads find the idea false. They say, 'Sure it's hard. But my children make me happy. Just look at my Instagram.'

I went back to the research. It showed a persistent relationship between childrearing and lower wellbeing.

I conducted my own studies with around 1000 Australian parents. The pattern remained. The research (my own and others) shows that parents experience lowered wellbeing as their children get older, and as they have more of them. Yet when I shared this research with parents of children of all ages, and from families both large and small, they assured me that the data were wrong. Or at least, it wasn't true for them.

In her acclaimed book *All Joy and No Fun*, journalist Jennifer Senior writes that 'most mothers and fathers rate parenting as their greatest joy'. She further explains that parents appear to be 'both happier and more miserable than nonparents', because parenting evokes a profound range of emotions, 'stressing its participants to their limits, no matter how much they love their children'.

(An important aside: researchers have found that children are more likely to think that they *cause* their mother's sadness and anger than her happiness. This may be because we show our anger strongly, clearly and memorably. Often our delight goes unexpressed – or at least we don't show our delight as obviously. We need to be sure that they know we delight in them, and show our joy more readily.)

A meaningful life is not a happy life ... until it is

What this means is that the daily drama of dealing with our daughter or son reduces our happiness. We don't tend to feel joy while separating squabbling siblings or picking up toys, wiping yogurt out of our carpet or arguing with a three-year-old about whether the seatbelt needs to go on or not.

These things try us. They stretch us. Our children call on us to improve ourselves *so that we can help them better.* These experiences bind us to our children. We respond to them because we love them. And because we love them, these tasks become both frustrating and mundane, *but also meaningful.* This is the key to the parenting paradox (of children making us miserable yet bringing us joy).

Meaning seems to be a better test of happiness than happiness itself. Professor of Psychology at Florida State University Roy Baumeister said, 'Parenthood may be a poor strategy for finding happiness, but an excellent one for achieving a meaningful life.'

Meaning doesn't necessarily make us happy in the moment (although it can). But as we look back at the meaningful things we have done – the giving, the effort, the sacrifice and even the tears – we experience amazing purpose and satisfaction.

This is where we experience joy.

So does this mean that family life is supposed to be hard until the children are gone? Are we supposed to be miserable until finally we get to the end and look back and feel happy? A famous quote counsels, 'Call no man happy until he is dead.' Depressing huh?

I don't believe that's a recipe for living with joy in our families.

This entire book has been about how we can make the effort, the sacrifice and the giving meaningful and purposeful.

And much of it is hard. Surprisingly, this hard work and challenge does make us happy – though not always in the moment.

But this chapter is less about the hard stuff and about more about finding joy in the small moments. And it's about helping our child find joy – real joy – in their lives. Because if childhood should be about anything, it should be about finding and experiencing joy.

As parents, by example and through teaching, our children need us to help them recognise and celebrate joy, and help them to cultivate joy.

How do we do that?

Recognising and celebrating joy

I was going to call this chapter, *Stop being a grumpy stresshead and make life fun!* because when I watch parents engaging with their children, I rarely see them smiling. In the shops, at the park … it's all business and seriousness. I can only imagine what it's like at home. And it's completely understandable. Life is busy. We have work commitments, there are bills to pay, we need to be somewhere almost all the time and the truth is that our children add huge pressure to our lives in many situations. But finding joy appears to be easiest when we set aside that to-do list and enjoy the moment.

Perhaps your child spills some milk. Rather than being upset about it, draw some fun shapes and see how milk responds to a finger rushing through it. Then work together when it is time to clean it up, and ask what alternative places (or ways) we might play next time. When one of our children was three, we went on a weekend getaway and forgot her shoes. We bought a nice pair of new shoes for her, and within ten minutes of putting them on her feet she had jumped into a big puddle. We could have been upset. Instead, we saw the delight in her eyes and let her play in the puddle for another ten minutes. The shoes were wet anyway! Those experiences of joy can be an important developmental marker to indicate that our child has made a crucial discovery. It is far better to enjoy it with them than to usher them quickly towards the domesticated.

Often, we want our children to be civilised and tidy. That puts us at odds with them. They want experience: wild and unscripted. We can enjoy it with them – safely – or we can try to prevent their access to joy. I remember leaving swimming lessons with a five-year-old one afternoon. (She was mine. I hadn't taken a random child.) As we passed the garden I turned back to see why my daughter wasn't beside me. We were late. I was frustrated. This was no time for dawdling. And then I noticed her bending over and smelling the flowers. My heart melted. She reminded me that there is joy in every moment if we look. We spent about 20 seconds looking at and smelling the flowers. Her curiosity was satisfied. And she gladly accompanied me to the car. Imagine the alternative! Slowing down creates opportunities for joy – and sometimes it only takes 20 seconds.

If you want to find ways to have more joy with your children, watch grandparents. Maturity (and, in some cases, retirement) allows them both more time and improved priorities. They celebrate joy with their grandchildren far better than parents. There may be something in that.

Perhaps we can both encourage our children to spend more time with their grandparents (or vice versa) *and* adopt their approach to priorities and relationships. When time is running out, we tend to focus more on what matters most.

There are significant and important things that we can do to increase our joy – and our children's joy – in our families. We can do the following – and many more.

Spend time together
Relationships are at the centre of our happiness and joy. When our relationships are strong and thriving, our joy fills up. Spending time with the people you love is a sure-fire way to increase joy for you and for them.

Hug
Hug lots. Touch, squeeze, be close. Hold those hugs for as long as the child wants to be hugged. Long hugs are way better than short hugs. Long hugs create a burst of the 'love' neurotransmitter oxytocin. They boost dopamine and serotonin. These are brain chemicals that promote bonding and positivity.

Spend time in nature
Nature is fuel for the soul. In nature we are more inclined to talk and connect, to be grateful and to be active. Time in nature promotes gratitude and awe, respect and reverence and a sense that there is something that transcends us and our often trivial daily dramas.

Serve
As a family, find people to serve. Do 'good deeds' for fun. Offer surprises and secret treats to neighbours and friends. Cook a meal for someone who is struggling. Let your child participate in your efforts. These acts of service strengthen your family and make everyone feel better about life.

Be grateful

As we appreciate the good things we have in life, research confirms that our sense of wellbeing and joy is increased. Being miserly and ungrateful reduces happiness and joy. Finding something to appreciate about challenges is tougher, but offers a sense of meaning and purpose.

Slow down

Can we stop being so busy? And can we also stop pretending that we're so busy because we are always engaged by our screens? Slow down, sit quietly, be available and create 'margin' in your life. Margin is that space on the page where there is room for notes and corrections. Margin is that space in our lives where there is room for other people and the possibility of change.

Play

When we play, we communicate, meet one another's gaze, listen, learn, establish rules, build relationships and become open to possibilities and influence. Our emotions stabilise. We learn to regulate behaviours. And we laugh.

We can find joy – and fun – in all kinds of inconvenient times and places. Children are most likely to recognise and celebrate joy when they are:

- With people they love doing things they like

- Doing something that energises them

- Curious

- Playing

- Developing mastery

Think about the breathtaking joy you feel in the following experiences:

- Watching your child sleep peacefully

- Experiencing one of those hugs where they snuggle right in

- Seeing your child engaged in some kind of activity, oblivious to the world

- Having a conversation with your three-year-old and realising that they *really* are talking with you

- Singing out loud to your child's favourite music as it plays full bore in the car

- Hearing your child tell you about something they've achieved

And so many more things. What are some of the experiences that bring you joy with your children?

These things, when we are fully in the moment, bring us joy. They bring our children joy. When we share them, our family joy is increased!

But how often do these simple things escape our attention? How easy is it to miss the joy in the moment because of our agenda, or our exhaustion or our busy schedule? It's too easy to tuck the kids into bed, walk out of the room, turn off the light and walk away without another thought when life gets pressured.

Savouring the small and mundane gives us access to, and awareness of, joy that is all too easy to miss in the busyness of family life.

I asked parents on my Facebook page to share the ways that they experience joy with their children. Within 20 minutes I had more than 100 responses, including:

- Sharing new experiences ... first time at the movies and first time riding our bikes at dusk to buy dinner were recent ones we loved. The kids felt so big and so independent.

- Hearing their thoughts and working-outs of the world around them. The way their brains work is so fascinating.

- Sharing in their joy when they discover little things I've forgotten to notice.

- When they randomly tell me 'I love you' and it's not a reply to me saying I love them. They initiate it.

- Watching them show genuine love and affection to one another. These are my favourite moments. I love hearing their laughter and funny conversations without any bickering or whining: just smiles and happiness.

- When they make a hard choice because it's the right thing to do, even when they don't want to or a friend is pressuring them to do something else.

- Hearing them sing and role-play when they think no one is watching.

- Seeing them act like kids, with the freedom to play. That childhood innocence is something to keep as long as possible.

One mum shared that for her it was the 'grounding moments' that brought the biggest and most unexpected joys. She stated: 'there are those times where we think we should be doing something else (housework, admin tasks, work stuff) and the children show us the pure joy that comes from just enjoying the moment and not worrying about anything else.'

Finding joy in family life isn't just about having fun – although fun is often experienced as a side-effect of joy. Studies show that some of the greatest joy in life comes, not from getting things, but from giving things. Here are three things you and your family can give to counter-intuitively find more joy:

Give time

You might give time to one another. Perhaps you will give time to friends or others you care for: neighbours and loved ones. Encouraging children to spend time with their grandparents, aunts, uncles and cousins is important for creating a sense of family and personal identity. These experiences promote joy and build lifelong memories and relationships. Children are wired to connect with others – especially extended family.

Give forgiveness

Holding on to grudges and anger is a certain way to find misery. When a child upsets you, forgive them quickly and restore the relationship. Be kind and humble, and remember that once upon a time you were a child who did awful things. (Maybe not awful like your child is doing … but awful nonetheless.)

Give hope

Kids who are hopeful are happier. They are more satisfied with life. They even do better with things like academic and athletic achievement and success. Hopeful kids have better relationships.

And if you don't have hope, well, you're hope-less. That's related to all the things we don't want for our children. Hopeless kids don't try, have poor relationships and feel helpless. They don't achieve goals, often because they don't set any. And when they do set them, that's where it stops, because they don't have enough hope to find ways to achieve those goals.

Parents who want to instil hope in their children can try the following three ideas.

1. **Build a future focus.** Speak to your children about what they're looking forward to in the next week, the next month and even the next year. If they're a little older, you might even ask them about bigger questions like 'What do you want to be as a grown-up?' Ask them what they want to have, do and be.

2. **Work with them on plans (or pathways).** When a child says, 'I want to be a marine biologist,' be encouraging and then ask them, 'What do you think we could do this week to help you learn more about marine biology? Where can we go to learn more about the ocean?' Discuss pathways, options and possibilities. Thinking about the future and making plans is central in fostering hope.

3. **Inspire with questions.** When they're stuck, rather than giving them an answer, ask them, 'What do you think is the next best thing to do?' or 'When have you overcome something like this before?'
   These types of questions promote a sense of agency or efficacy. Rather than having our children rely on us for all of the answers, they can rely on themselves, their resourcefulness and their initiative. They can recall times that they've succeeded before and use that to build hope that they can succeed again.

As parents, our wish for our children is that they will grow up happy and resilient. Our wish can become 'hope' when we use these three keys to build hope in them as they look towards the future.

———————————————

Stacey came to a parenting presentation I ran, and shared the following story with me on Facebook a few days later.

Last night I went out on a rare date with my husband. Early dinner and a movie. When we got home I went into my daughter's bedroom. She was still awake so I sat with her and we had a brief chat. I was heading to bed when she asked if we could play a game of cards.

My eyes were hanging out of my head. It was past her bedtime. I was ready to sleep. It was on the tip of my tongue to say no. But I said yes. We had fun. And she won best out of five!

While we were playing, there was a little bit of chatter, a little bit of laughter and a lot of frenzied competition. She said to me, 'Mum, this is more fun than being on my device.'

Her words, her smile and her laughter made me glad I stayed up to hang out with her, even if I did get my backside kicked. She hardly every plays cards with me. And it was a fabulous night, even if we were exhausted. I don't think I would have said yes if I hadn't been to your seminar and heard you talk. I would have gone to bed and missed that connection with my girl.

Dessert brings joy

When was the last time you let the kids eat dessert first? How long has it been since you rolled around on the floor and wrestled? Have you taken a Friday off work, pulled the children out of kindy or preschool or class, and gone somewhere for fun just because you can? Or perhaps just stood and stared at the precious child who has fallen asleep somewhere bizarrely uncomfortable and thought, How did I make someone so perfect?

It's one thing to experience joyful things. It's another thing to experience joy.

Experience has shown me that we all too easily miss the things that bring us joy. They are all around us. But when we stop, look and listen – when we are truly present and mindful (rather than mind-full) – we both cultivate and recognise joy, and family life becomes joyful. Yes, it will remain challenging. It will continue to stretch us. But finding the joy will allow us to appreciate the stretching and personal growth.

As our kids see joy they relax. They like being with us. Life is good.

936 is not very much

Some years ago I made a count of the number of weekends we get with our children, as long as all goes well. If there are 52 weekends each year and our children are 'children' for 18 years, the sum total of weekends we have to spend with them is 936.

936.

Of course, we won't get all 936 of them. Work, sport, family commitments and so many other things get in the way. Reminding ourselves of this makes it easier to remember how important it is to make the most of most moments.

This highlights the importance of getting our priorities in order. As we decide how to spend time as a family, we have decisions to make to determine what is going to be best for individuals as well as the whole family unit. I love the idea I heard in a conference years ago, in the talk 'Good, Better, Best', that we should be careful not to exhaust our available time on things that are merely good and leave little time for that which is better or best. The speaker shared an example of how tricky – and how simple – getting this right can be. A friend of his took his young family on a holiday. They visited attractions, historical sites and beautiful natural 'wonders'. After the holiday, he asked his son what his favourite part of the holiday had been. 'What I enjoyed most,' the boy replied, 'was when it was just you and me and we lay on the lawn and looked at the stars and talked.'

The conference speaker then made his final point: amazing family activities may be good for children, but they are not always better than one-on-one time with a loving parent.

In our family, we have a 'Super-Saturday' tradition of spending time as a family in low-cost or no-cost activities. We are creative, we go and explore places and our children generally enjoy the chance to do this. But we have also come to realise that while those weekends are limited, and they vanish at a remarkable rate, the one-on-one times we get with our kids may be even more challenging to find and make the most of. We have learned that the car drives, the quiet nights sitting on the edge of the bed, around the dinner table: these are some of the best times for us to really engage with, find joy with and experience delight with our children.

There are countless practical ways that we can invite joy into our children's lives. Which of the following could work for your family?

- Take regular camping trips

- Create a slip 'n' slide in your backyard

- Lie on the grass and stare at clouds

- Race to the shops for a treat together

- Play cards or board games

- Read a favourite story

- Visit a relative or tell a story about an ancestor

- Do chores together (Yes. Seriously. It's fun when we work side by side.)

- Ride a bike, visit a park, go for a walk (Yes, it's hard. But it's always worth it.)

Do you think that getting everyone together to hang out in the living room and watch YouTube videos will be a highlight you'll reflect on with joy in years to come?

Make evenings a time of nurture and joy

The most important relationship children will have for at least the first dozen years of their lives will be what they share with their parents. And night-time seems to be one of the best times to nurture that relationship.

Somewhere between the deadlines and demands we each face, we can find ourselves wondering whether the stresses of being a parent ever end. Well, yes, they do, albeit briefly. Most often, they end somewhere between 7 pm and 9 pm each night when the kids finally fall asleep and we get a few brief moments of adult time as the day closes.

How do you approach the moments before your kids go to sleep? Is it chaos followed by relief? Or is it a time of quiet connection that strengthens your relationships? I believe that if we focus on five central conversations at night-time, we and our children will feel more joy. I call this 'night-time nurture'.

1. What was great today?

People who are genuinely appreciative of the good things in their lives are happy – and happy people find lots to be grateful for. In my family, talking about our 'grateful things' has become an evening staple, and our children rattle off their lists with delight. We have been struck with our children's insights when they have shared sad or difficult things they are grateful for because of the learning or growth that came out of challenge.

2. What are you looking forward to?

In *The Optimistic Child*, Professor Martin Seligman identifies this question as a personal favourite because it points children towards a positive future. He points out that hope and optimism are powerful deterrents to depression. Plus, we get to be excited with them as they look forward to positive events.

3. Is there anything you want to talk about?

I have been amazed at the revelations my children have shared when they know they have my full focus and attention. This question has led to conversations about experiences and emotions, and fears and worries that I would never have known about or been able to share in had I not taken a few moments to ask.

There have been very few times when my children have said, 'Nope. Nothing to talk about.' Instead, it seems that they crave opportunities to connect with us, as their parents.

4. I'm sorry

If, during the course of the day, we have not been our best selves, this final few minutes together is a valuable time to make much needed relationship repairs. Letting our children know we are sorry for not being our best teaches leadership, humility and humanity, and it shows a willingness to put the relationship ahead of frustrations and grudges.

5. I love you

This statement, heartfelt and meaningful, matters more than anything. Say it every night. Make sure it is accompanied by a hug and kiss – or the expression of love that is most meaningful to your child.

Honest, caring listening may be the most important thing we can do to show our kids we care about them, and to help them really feel it. Those final minutes each night can be a precious – almost sacred – time of listening, repair and love. And as our child falls asleep in our embrace and we softly leave the room, the feeling that we experience in our hearts is the purest joy there is.

Finding joy when there is no joy to be found

A cruel challenge of family life is that while we all want our family to be happy, much of the time most of our families will encounter pain and trial. We might experience grief and loss. Children may be ill or experience learning difficulties or other developmental challenges. Partners may fight and separate. Sons and daughters may long for an absent parent. Or children may behave rebelliously, choosing to ignore our requests. (This last challenge becomes particularly prominent in the middle teen years.) Sometimes, we're simply exhausted with the ongoing demands of young children who rely on us for so much.

Sometimes, family life leaves us feeling miserable and without hope. Are we supposed to just smile and 'find joy' anyway?

This question gets at the very core of what family is about. Everyone has different ideas of what family should be about – and this drives expectations for how families should function. I believe that families are not just the vehicles for children to be born and socialised – although that is a central reason we have families. I see families as incredible structures that promote personal progress and development.

Humans are, I believe, born with an inbuilt desire to grow, discover, learn and improve. I can't think of a single person I've spoken to about 'life' who has said, 'You know what. I'm complete. I'm satisfied. I'm not interested in doing more, being more or having more.' We *all* want to be better. It's a human *thing*. And families are the *best* place for us to learn to be better. Thus, I believe that when awful, challenging, traumatic experiences occur – the ones that leave us reeling, that break our hearts and that cause us to question everything about who we are, what we believe and what we really want in life – they are perfectly designed to teach us to be better people.

When we respond with patience and gentleness to a sick and screaming infant who *will not sleep no matter what*, we become better people. When we respond to a challenging child who *will not listen to a word I say* with calm, consistent openness, acceptance and love (while still expressing our clear expectations in a loving way), we learn to be better people. When we respond with curiosity to a struggling child, when we respond with careful listening and compassion to a broken-hearted child, and when we respond with humility and a willingness to say sorry to a child we have wronged, we become bigger people. Indeed, when we respond with continued kindness and service to a child (or other family member) who really does not deserve it, we discover that there is more 'substance to our soul'. We become more significant and more influential in the eyes of those we love and serve. And ironically, while not seeking it, those experiences bring us greater joy than they otherwise would – both in the moment, and in years to come as we look at the way we have been refined in what can sometimes be the furnace of family life.

Take-home message

Most of us experience moments of extraordinary joy when our children are young. We seem to be a little less good at finding those moments as our children get to about age three. By the time they're in their teens, it's even harder. It gets messy in those middle years (from 3 to 23). But there is joy everywhere throughout our parenting lives if we're looking. We are also excellent at finding joy when everyone is happy and life is peaceful. These are joyful times. But there are times when joy is hard to find. Family life tries us. In those moments, we grow the most – if we are open to growth. And we find joy. Maybe that mix of joy and growth is exactly what we need?

Robert Louis Stevenson said, 'For to miss the joy is to miss all.'

10

Getting support as a parent

In *The 7 Habits of Highly Effective People*, the late Dr Stephen R Covey described a crucial habit for effectiveness. He called it 'sharpen the saw'. Dr Covey described two men cutting down trees. One of them began each day by spending some time sharpening his axe or saw. The other man got straight to work. 'I've got too many trees to chop down to do something silly like that!'

Yet it was the man who took time out to sharpen his saw who was more effective. Covey asks whether you've ever been driving along and seen the car is nearly out of fuel. Would you say to yourself, 'Haven't got time to stop for fuel. Too busy going places!'?

We need to take time out to refuel, to sharpen the saw. We need to renew our resolve and refresh our goals. And, as parents, we need to recruit others to our cause – particularly our partners.

This chapter is about finding support so that we can be our best as parents.

At the start of this book I emphasised the importance of working with your partner and being on the same page. My sense is that most people know *what* they need to do. But *how* to do it is the challenge. I hear statements like this all the time.

Parent: I know I'm supposed to be patient with my child, but *how* do I do it when I've asked a thousand times and I feel like I should not need to be patient any more?

Parent: I know I need to avoid punishment by working with my child, but *how* do I do it when their obstinate refusal to interact with me means we can't progress?

Parent: I know we're supposed to be on the same page, but *how* do I convince my partner that we can do things differently when I barely know how to do it myself?

Date night

To move you close to being on the same page, we're going to get you dating again. (When I say dating *again* let me be clear: I'm talking about dating the other adult or co-parent/s you raise your children with!)

Presumably you dated back in the good old days before you got together, made serious commitments to one another and had children. Hopefully you liked dating because it's about to become part of the routine for a while as you sharpen that parenting saw.

Currently single?

Don't let singlehood stop you. You can still go on a date. Call a girlfriend or ring a mate – or go out with your new flame. Take your parents out. Give them a copy of this book so you can work through it together.

The purpose of the dates? You have work to do. This is where we move from *what* to do through to *how* we're going to do it. Dates are not just about watching movies any more. Date night is about having the conversations, doing the work and learning together.

If you aren't in a trusting relationship, I get that you might be in circumstances where you don't feel comfortable talking about all the personal stuff that parenting brings up with someone else. If that's you, don't sweat it. While the date night part of the book is set up as conversations between two, you can totally do it on your own. Collaborating on this hard work may be easier for most people though. It's good to know someone's in your corner and has your back.

How you do date night is up to you. You may be single or in a relationship but prefer to do something in a group. If you're more into group gatherings, let me suggest that the ideas in this book would make for an awesome group date or book club conversation. Don't be limited by narrow thinking. Go with what is going to bring the best value and improvement into your life. Heck, you might even want to make it a family date night! Bring the children in on your conversations. (I should add that if there is any ambivalence or friction in your conversations, it is probably best to process this without the children being present. Some of them may use this as leverage to manipulate situations for their gain. Others may feel insecure when parents appear unsure or misaligned.)

The most important thing is that you block out a time every week to work through the activities in this chapter. Each week, go on a date or have the parenting conversation. You'll note that each date outline in this chapter corresponds with a chapter in the book. Do a quick refresh on the chapter, have the conversations and make the changes that will help you be the parent you want to be.

'Why can't I just read the book?'

- First, spending time and connecting in meaningful relationships is the foundation of wellbeing and a healthy psychological and emotional life. These dates will help you to connect. They'll centre and balance you individually, as a couple, or as a group. Time together *should*, under normal circumstances, make you happier. (Fingers crossed.)

- Second, it creates unity. There may be nothing more powerful in parenting than being prepared, forearmed and united in a consistent approach as you tackle the challenges your children present. Once you've talked things through, you're ready for whatever the children throw your way, regardless of whether you're reading this in a couple relationship, as a single parent relying on extended family support or a group of like-minded parents working together to make your families happier.

  After 20 years of marriage, raising six children (the oldest is now 18 and finished high school), and having worked with so many couples who are doing battle with each other *as well as their children*, I *know* that being on the same page as your significant other (or at least being consistent) is as important as anything else you can name in a family. When Kylie and I are in harmony, we're unstoppable. When we're not in sync, the conflict and division escalate fast.

- Third, talking aloud about ideas seems to clarify our thinking and lead to new ideas that are better than anything we might have thought of without talking it through. We see new possibilities, identify gaps in our plans and, so long as the conversation is civil, get to provide and receive input from someone who cares about the issues as much as we do.

Making it happen

So, now that you know date nights are coming, let's work out the logistics because *that* can be the toughest part.

Each week for the next nine weeks you'll be calling in the babysitters and going on a date to talk about your parenting and your family. I know sometimes there are no grandparents nearby and budgets can be an issue. Babysitters can be expensive! There are creative ways around this.

In the early years of our marriage, Kylie and I used to go on a date one week while our friends would help us by minding the children. They had their own children to deal with during our date night, and so to get around that small obstacle he would stay home with his children while she would come to our place and put our children to bed. To make it fair, the following week we would swap. You might have a neighbour with a child old enough to babysit and score a few dollars. Be creative. But go out on a weekly date and talk about this stuff. There are ten things to talk about (including this one). That means ten date nights over the next ten weeks. It will change your family.

And if date night is honestly and completely impractical, stay up on Friday night once the children are in bed and have some treats to make it feel like a date. Spend some dollars on something you love to eat or drink, and enjoy. For Kylie and me, it's some fancy cheese and crackers. For you it might be a wine or coffee, or perhaps some chocolate, raspberries and ice-cream. Go with what works for you. But make it feel like a date.

One more thing: these date nights don't have to be the same night every week. Some people do shift work or FIFO. Sometimes things come up. The main thing is that you're having genuine couple time about once a week, during which you can talk about your parenting and your children. It's these date nights that will get you parenting on the same page. They're about communication, being clear on values and discussing direction. There is tremendous power in unity, and both you and your children will feel it. On the flipside, there is despondency and defeat in division. The family will feel that even more.

When you're parenting on the same page you'll be compatible. Our children *need* parents who are singing from the same hymnbook. Lessons taught consistently cut through and are lasting, but lessons taught inconsistently are rarely effectively learned. (As an important aside, sometimes consistency can be hard to achieve. In such cases, work on cooperation. Dad may agree to give Mum's approach a try for a week and see how that works. Enduring differences can be hard to overcome, so date night might become, in some cases, a negotiation around cooperation.

Okay, so weekly date nights are scheduled for whatever night works best.

_____

What night is your next date night? _____

Who is watching the children?_____

Where are you going? _____

What time? _____

Are you both ready to talk about important family stuff?   Yes   No

Remember to take pen and paper!

_____

Date night 1:
Parenting on the same page

Your first date night involves a conversation with a handful of talking points. Like I said before, don't worry about where the date is. Just make sure you have it. At home is fine if you can't get out. Once the children are in bed, order your favourite takeaway, organise your favourite drink and dessert, hop into something comfortable and begin. Make it special.

For date night number one, we're doing some family planning. Not the kind that revolves around deciding the number of children we'll welcome. Instead, this is about working out how we want our family to be.

Have a chat with your partner about what you really want for your family. Don't just say, 'to be happy'. That's too vague. Instead, think about the questions below and use them as a guide for what your family might look like.

These simple questions can help you get on the same page when it comes to what you want for your family!

1. What memories do you cherish most from your childhood?

2. How would you like your children to remember their childhoods?

3. What can we do to make that more likely?

There's one final question to begin discussing, but you may not come up with an immediate answer. It's this:

4. When it comes to your children, what's your end goal for them? What is it that you want most for them?

In relation to this question, I love what esteemed parenting author Haim Ginott suggested. We want to raise children who are strong and caring. Strength connotes responsibility, independence, capacity and industry. These are wonderful attributes, but when a person is too strong and lacking in care or compassion, they may trample over others, only focus on their own needs and otherwise miss opportunities to contribute. By being strong *and* caring, they are able to fend for themselves *and* care for others. I think this is a valuable combination of characteristics.

My other end goal for my children is that they discover who they truly are and can be. I want them to have vision and the courage to go in directions that feel authentic and true to who they are.

Of course, you may have an entirely different and equally worthwhile goal for your children. The main point here is to discuss and consider what you're really aiming to achieve with your children.

As we work through the remaining dates, you may find that the answer to this question may be *the thing* that you need most to guide your parenting. Be open to your plans changing as you discover more. (And be prepared to bring older children in to the conversation. Their insights can help.)

Date night 2: Mattering and belonging

Now that you're heading in the same direction, it's time to focus on how well we're paying attention to the children.

Here are some conversation starters:

1. Were there any remarks in Chapter 2 that struck a chord with you? Why? What insights did you gain that could guide decisions in your family?

2. Take a minute to think of a time when someone was completely available for you. How did it feel? Think of a time when you were entirely available for your children. How did it feel? How was it received?

3. Discuss ways that you make yourself available to your children. Which ways feel most authentic for you? What works best for the children?

4. Map out a loose plan for sharing one-on-one time with your children.

Some ideas to help you engage with your children this week might include the following.

- Express affection and compassion more.
- Plan and engage in activities that bring mutual enjoyment with your children.
- Tell your children you love them.
- Stop, look and listen.
- Stop, drop and roll.

- Write a love note to your child and put it in their lunchbox or under their pillow.
- Go for a walk or a bike ride.
- Take the time to talk with children to help them to feel significant.
- Read books together – that they choose (and read slowly, especially if they're young).

5. What is one activity you might plan for this week? How can you be more aware of times for fun together?

6. Talk about the three central obstacles that you think interrupt your availability. Pick one or two – but no more – that you think you could work on this week to create more emotional availability in your home.

7. How can you support one another to be available to your children (and to one another) without getting on each other's case?

Date night 3:
Being understood

On your date night this week, take a few minutes to discuss each of your children individually. Talk about how they're doing, the things they've been sharing with you, what they seem to be enjoying about life, what their strengths are and what you think could be worrying them. Look to see how much your partner can teach you – and identify what you might have missed.

Dr John Gottman suggests we turn towards our children and their emotions rather than turning away from them or turning against them. When we turn against, we disapprove. We get mad. We become frustrated. We blame our children. When we turn away, we dismiss. We ignore. We tell them not to worry because it's not a big deal.

When we turn towards, we recognise they are acting in a way that makes sense to them and that if we don't understand their actions we are simply lacking information. We begin a process of discovery where we see their emotions and behaviour as a chance to connect, to be together, to teach and to build them – and our relationships with them.

Discuss one example of each of these alternatives you have personally experienced with your children in the past week. Make some notes about your observations in the space provided opposite.

Turning away

This week I turned away from _____

How did my child feel when I turned away? _____

How did I feel? _____

What was the outcome? _____

What was my child actually feeling? _____

What would it have looked like if I'd turned towards,

rather than away? _____

What would I have done? _____

What would I have said? _____

Turning against

This week I turned against _____

How did my child feel? _____

How did I feel? _____

What was the outcome? _____

What was my child actually feeling? _____

What would it have looked like if I'd turned towards,

rather than against? _____

What would I have done? _____

What would I have said? _____

Turning towards

This week I turned towards _____

How did my child feel? _____

How did I feel? _____

What was the outcome? _____

Date night 4:
Something better than punishment

Rules without relationships lead to rebellion. The purpose of the chapters about belonging and understanding is to create a relationship foundation for you and for your children. Without this foundation, rules feel horrible. They feel like control.

Now that your relationship is strengthening, it's time to get into the limit-setting, teaching aspect of working with our children. This can be an area fraught with tension as stressed parents attempt to influence their children's challenging behaviour in different ways.

These questions will be useful in guiding your date-night conversation.

1. What were the typical 'discipline' strategies used in your home growing up, when you were a child?
   Why did your parents rely on those strategies?
   How did it feel for you when those strategies were used?
   To what extent did those strategies improve your behaviour (in the moment, in the short term and in the long term)?
   How did those strategies impact your relationship with your parents (in the moment, in the short term and in the long term)?

2. What are your typical 'go-to' discipline strategies in your home now, with your own children?
   Do your strategies involve much 'badge-showing'?

3. As you reflect on the kind of family you want to have (your vision), and the kind of people you all want to be (or the principles you want to live by), how do your typical 'discipline' strategies help you or hinder you?

4. Describe to one another your most profound and
positive discipline experiences with your children.

What were the circumstances?

How did you respond?

Did you deal with things in the moment, or wait until
everyone was calm?

Was there yelling and threats? Or was it a conversation
where you worked things out?

What made the discipline so *positive*?

How can you have more of those moments?

Think of an iceberg. There's a little bit of ice above the water. There's
lots of ice below. As I've said before, our children's challenging
behaviour is a lot like an iceberg. Think about the behaviours that your
child exhibits that are challenging. Write them above the waterline
in the illustration below. Now, discuss together all of the potential
unmet needs your child/ren may have that lead to those challenging
behaviours. For example, your child may come home in a cranky
mood after school. You may think he's tired. But perhaps a student or
teacher snubbed him?

Does your typical 'discipline' approach address the behaviours above
the water? Or the needs below the water?

Date night 5:
Getting along with others – including siblings!

The ideas in Chapter 5 can be challenging. They require us – and our children – to get out of BED (Blame, Excuse and Denial) and use our OAR (Ownership, Accountability and Responsibility). This means we have to acknowledge the part that *we* have played in conflicts with our children so we can teach them to take responsibility for their contributions.

For this date night, I suggest working through the vicious circle three times, in three different ways. This will help you understand it well enough to teach it. And it will help you guide your children through challenges and conflict.

Talking point 1

Think of a time where *you* have had a conflict with your child. Work through the vicious circle and see what insights you discover. Start by discussing what your child did that incensed you. Write it in the box. Then take a moment to recall your feelings. Next, note your actions. Finally, focus on how they felt when you behaved that way towards them.

You might do this once for a positive response and another time for a negative response. And you might also continue the circle further. Once you behaved that way towards them and they felt what they felt, how did they act? How did that make you feel?

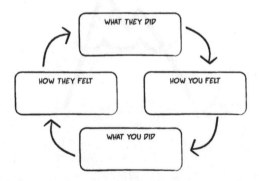

With your date-night partner, answer the following three questions:

1. Who started it?

   (Note: the answer is irrelevant, but it is designed to make us question whether it *really* was the other person or us.)

2. Who is contributing to the conflict?

3. Who is responsible for stopping the conflict?

Talking point 2

Now go through the exercise again using an alternative conflict situation, ideally related to a conflict between siblings.

Imagine what they would say as you interview them. Have your partner role-play with you and help resolve the conflict.

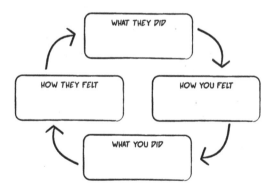

Talking point 3

If you want to go deeper and get more advanced, think of a personal conflict you might be experiencing with someone. Work through this vicious circle with openness and honesty.

Is there something *you* are doing that keeps you both in that circle?

What can you do to get out of it and move the relationship to a more positive place?

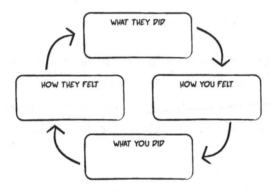

This is hard work. It demands ownership. It means we can't play the victim. And it requires that regardless of their response, we commit to acting in harmony with our deeply held values.

Date night 6: Discovering the self

If you are the parent of young children, guiding your child's self-discovery will not be high on your priority list. However, a quick Google will help you find a copy of Professor Marshall Duke's 'Do You Know' scale. I recommend finding it and discussing it with your partner and your children. It's fun, and it can begin a valuable process of identity development in your child.

For this week's date night, however, there are three talking points and a handful of fun questions to ask one another about your child – or your hopes and plans for your child if they're very young.

Talking point 1

Ask one another:

> What lights our children up?
> When do they come alive?
> What do they love to do?
> How can we facilitate opportunities for them to do
> more of this?

As we identify our children's strengths, we are more able to provide them with opportunities to find joy in their lives, develop competence and confidence and make a meaningful contribution.

Talking point 2

> Is there anything that we aspire to for our children
> that might be more about us than them?

Talking point 3

Rather than a discussion with your partner, plan a time for the following activity with your children.

If your children are at least seven or eight years old, look up Solomon Asch's experiment on conformity on the Internet. Gather the basic facts and talk to your children about the study. Ask them what they would do in the situation. (Don't do the experiment. It's unfair and unethical.) Do the same with Stanley Milgram's obedience study. (You may want to show them a YouTube clip, depending on their age.)

Use these studies as object lessons. Invite your children to consider how they would act before they knew about the experiment, and now that they do know. Then talk about similar situations at school or home where 'knowing who you are and what is right' might mean they act in a way that is non-conformist.

These conversations can be tricky. But they can also help children to think about who they are and who they want to be.

Date night 7:
Finding a balance with technology

This week's date night is as much about you as it is about your children. The purpose of this date night is to develop a family media plan.

The following questions will be useful.

1. What are the most positive screen and media experiences we have shared as a family? How can we encourage more of those experiences?

2. When is it appropriate to use media and screens? When do we require screen-free time?

3. What is our decision regarding filters and security measures?

4. What is our decision regarding the apps that our children will be allowed access to? And at what ages?

5. Where is it allowable for screens to be used? Where are screens not allowed?

6. How much screen time is reasonable? How will we encourage compliance?

7. What exceptions to the plan might be reasonable?

8. How can we set a positive and balanced example of technology use?

Once you are on the same page, some personal changes may be required. Discuss how you can support one another. And remember, if your children are going to be challenged by these changes, it may be useful to spend time explaining and exploring. You might even empower your children to make some decisions for themselves!

Date night 8: Protecting childhood

This date night is really about becoming ruthlessly protective of your child's childhood. It's about working out what will strengthen them and excite them – giving them play and development opportunities – and removing irrelevant and unhelpful stressors from their life.

There are some heavy conversation opportunities that can build out of this chapter. As with other dates, I'll provide a handful of talking points. Remember, the purpose of these conversations is not for you to agree with everything I have said. Rather, it's to help you become aligned and on the same page with one another, and find ways to cooperate as you work towards your big-picture goals for helping your child.

Talking point 1

Did you feel like you experienced much of a childhood? If no, why not? If yes, what made it feel so special? How can you provide your children with those magic childhood experiences based on play, freedom and space, time and carefree creativity?

Ideas might include:

- reading stories
- playing games
- riding bikes or going for walks
- building a cubby house or tree house
- having quiet time lying on the lawn staring at the sky
- visiting parks, beaches and mountain peaks

... and so many more that will resonate for you and your family.

Talking point 2

In terms of schooling, the following questions may be useful.

What is our position on school starting age?

Where do we stand on homework?

Do we feel that withdrawing our children from standardised testing is appropriate?

Talking point 3

What seems to be an appropriate amount of activities for our child to be involved in?

Are our children participating in them because they want to, or because we want them to?

How can we guide our children to activities that they love, and support them when it gets challenging?

Are competitive pursuits inspiring or demotivating our child?

Date night 9:
Feeling joy

For your final date night, I'm not going to give you much to do – except to have fun. Feel what it's like to laugh and enjoy one another's company. Talk about what you're grateful for. Focus on being in the moment. Savour the food, the conversation and the chance to be together.

You might also find it helpful to talk about ways you can feel more joy in your family. These might include sharing 'grateful things' around the dinner table, working together on a project or having fun activities together on weekends or after school and work. Perhaps it could be having a quiet moment with a challenging child where you simply stare into their eyes and tell them you are proud of them, and love them with an intensity you can't describe.

This week, find joy in all of those small moments. Oh ... and eat dessert first!

(Note: there is no Date Night 10 for supporting one another in parenting. The past nine date nights have been all about supporting one another, working together and finding ways to serve each other and your family. From now on, however, I hope you've created a new tradition and that you continue to have weekly date nights where you continue to support one another, follow your family plan and create more opportunities to give your children the foundations they need to thrive and flourish in their lives.)

Afterword

Aussie finance expert Scott Pape published a bestselling book in 2016 called *The Barefoot Investor*. In the introduction, Scott describes the day his family lost their Victorian bushland home to a fire. As they surveyed the damage, he was amazed that the fire's ferocity was so great it had consumed everything that was once his home.

In spite of the sorrow of losing it all, Scott said his first thought was: I've got this. He knew that, despite the drama, he had his financial security sorted and could get his family through.

I've thought a lot about that statement as it relates to parenting.

I've got this.

In the past two decades I have earned two psychology degrees, one of which was a PhD, and I've written four parenting books. I've written countless articles, given seminars to tens of thousands of parents and counselled innumerable mums and dads through caregiving crises. My wife and I have six children!

But with all that experience, I still don't feel like I can look at parenting with an 'I've got this' mentality. From time to time we all have good moments, but most parents readily confess that typically those moments are fleeting. Parenting feels a little less concrete than finances. And when we get too cocky and think we really have 'got this', one of the children develops an attitude, experiences some newfound growth, finds a new friend or habit and humbles us with disarming and clinical precision and incisiveness. From a two-year-old who will not play nice with a sibling to an eight-year-old who knows everything, to a teenager who reminds us we can't make them do anything at all, it seems most parents experience constant desperation and anxiety regarding *how* we should raise our children.

Making it up as we go along

As I said at the outset, the cliché is that our children don't come with an instruction manual. Of course there *are* books, textbooks, research papers and more that are designed to help us, but even these resources don't fully prepare us for the unique challenges our children bring us. I haven't yet come across a book that provides a step-by-step outline for how to respond when your three-year-old continually removes her clothes in public places, regardless of how many times you put them back on (or how many 'inescapable' clothing items you purchase), nor the best words to say to a nine-year-old whose spirit is being ground into the dust by bullies ... and so on.

We find ourselves frustrated as we tell our kids to get their feet off the food, get their underwear off their head or get their hands out of the biscuit tin. And there are those times when we are so frustrated with our children because they're *just like us*!

The more parents I've spoken to, the more certain I've become that we are all making it up as we go along. We can use the valuable principles this book describes to aid us on our journey, but we have to constantly adapt them to circumstances we don't expect to face and cannot plan for.

The final thing we need to know

This eternal fear of getting it wrong leads me to the final thing that needs to be said to conclude this book. In addition to the big ideas I've shared, there is one more thing that I believe *every* parent needs to know when it comes to childrearing.

You *are* good enough.

As a parent who is intentional and devoted, you will feel like a failure a lot. It is inescapable. You will be your own worst critic. Now and then others might criticise you as well – even if they are well meaning. Your partner might point out a parenting failure. Your parents (or in-laws) or your own children may also highlight a hypocrisy or inconsistency.

You'll say you don't care, but it still hurts. Some days will be worse than others. But that feeling of inadequacy, the never-ending question of 'am I enough?', will be present persistently. There will be things that trigger the feeling: that time you shouted, the time you are so mad you call your child a name, the regrettable moment you snap and lash out physically. Then there's the day your child says or does something you find vile, the feelings of helplessness when you discover your child has been lying or stealing for some time, or the day you find that in spite of all your teaching and forewarning, your child has been exposed to pornography – or has even started consuming it regularly. Sometimes you'll question whether you're enough because of a child's wilful rebellion in spite of your most persistent and loving teaching.

You will feel like you have failed. It is inescapable. And because your child is not perfect, you'll be upset – perhaps at your child, but almost certainly at yourself. These feelings are normal. But I fear that whenever we use another person's behaviour as an indicator of our personal worth, we're being unfair to ourselves. Yes, even when that person is our child.

So let me be clear, once again. *You are enough.*

You need to believe that. Especially when things aren't going well. I believe that rather than judging ourselves as parents by the way our children turn out – which is to ignore the fact that our children have agency, or the ability to choose how they'll behave regardless of what we say – we are best to base our judgement on the fact that we keep on trying. Trying to help them *and* trying to be better parents.

When they're driving us mad do we keep trying to improve things? Maybe we lick our wounds for a while, but we return with our best efforts to be patient and kind.

Yes, parenting *is* about raising great kids. But we can't always control the outcomes. Even if we fully discharge our responsibility to our children (and to society) by teaching and socialising our children well, some of them will still choose to ignore us. What will we do then? For me, that is the measure of what kind of parent we are.

Our role as parents is to help, lift and encourage growth in our children. We are here to replace fear, anxiety and discouragement with hope and joy. How do we do that?

We practise the ideas in this book. We teach with love. We respond to challenge with kindness. We show patience when we want to explode. We remember that they're only little. They're learning. They need us to teach them.

With this view in mind, we become kinder – to our children and to ourselves. We recognise parenting is also about helping the parent grow.

Giving our hearts

In the novel *Ninety-Three*, French writer Victor Hugo wrote:

> She broke the bread into two fragments and gave them to her children, who ate with eagerness.
> 'She hath kept none for herself,' grumbled the sergeant.
> 'Because she is not hungry,' said a soldier.
> 'No,' said the sergeant, 'because she is a mother.'

It is almost impossible to put into words the depth of love that we feel as parents towards our children. As Cordelia explains in Shakespeare's *King*

Lear, when speaking of her love for her parent, 'My love's … richer than my tongue … I cannot heave my heart into my mouth.'

If you feel that way towards your children, then you are enough. The endless laundry, the thankless tasks related to maintaining your home, the challenges children provide: each compounds to make us feel like it might all be too much. And Instagram makes it look like everyone else is doing it so well! They get their pre-baby body back in five weeks, their meals all look like they've come from a hatted restaurant kitchen and they seem to have so much more time to spend doing meaningful activities with their children. The surest way to feel poorly about your parenting is to compare yourself with others, especially when you mostly only get to see their highlights reel.

Parenting is as much about the good times on Instagram as it is about those moments you would never want anyone to see. It's about how we respond to the runny noses, the fussy eating, the wet beds, the soiled underwear or the puddle on the carpet that provides evidence that the toilet training still has a way to go. It's about how we respond to the complaints that 'my legs are sore and I can't walk' on tired mornings, the lost school jumpers and the never-ending sibling challenges that confront every parent of more than one child. Our responses to those micro-moments that occur endlessly, day in and day out, set the foundation for our children's lives.

As you respond with patience, kindness, understanding, compassion and a desire to help rather than hurt, you're doing enough. You're doing all that is required. You are growing. You are loving. And *you are enough as a parent*. You are doing work that will never be seen by anyone beyond your family, but the value of that foundation you lay will last for generations.

You are important

Every one of us looks to our parents as someone important in our lives. Regardless of whether our parents were perfect or pathetic, they are important to us. Their behaviour and their love (or lack thereof) impact us every day.

I feel dreadfully sorry for my parents. Their son is a 'parenting expert'. We've had several conversations over the years about how they raised me and my siblings. They've genuinely inquired as to how they could have done things differently? Better?

I've been hesitant to highlight their failings. Why? Because they know (and I know) that they are imperfect people, and I don't want to point out all the stuff they did that was 'wrong'. They were doing the best they knew how to do and, as an adult child, I *cherish* their efforts. I forgive them for their mistakes, as most of us do for our parents. Children, us and ours, are remarkably forgiving. And that is because of that wiring that makes almost all of us want to be close to our parents. (Plus, it makes Christmas and other family gatherings much more bearable when we forgive, love and connect!)

Parents are important. Perhaps parents are the most important people in our lives. And we are truly *that* important to our children. Perhaps this feels like a burden at times. But I want to spin this around and highlight the incredible opportunity that it represents. *You are enough to your child because you are so important to your child.* Yes, it's true that there's always more to do. We can always be better. That's life. Don't let that be a burden. Instead, see it as an opportunity for constant growth and improvement.

Your kids love you. They are biologically designed to love you and to look at you with admiration and a desire to follow you and be connected to you.

You can do this

I have a novel way of teaching my children to ride their bikes. I take the pedals off the bike, put them on the bike seat, ensuring that their feet can touch the ground, and I ask them to use their feet to push themselves along. It doesn't take long before they gather momentum and feel comfortable balancing while they 'scoot'.

After about an hour of this I put the pedals back on the bike. We walk to a very gentle rise and I put my child on the bike again. This time I ask them to put their feet on the pedals and, with a gentle push, they roll down the hill. (We've mapped out where they should steer ahead of time.) I encourage them to pedal. Typically, my children have mastered the balancing and pedalling parts of riding their bike within a few minutes.

Now and then, a child has fallen. They've grazed their knee and they've come to me, tears rolling down their faces. I've given them a cuddle and a kiss. I've offered some gentle encouragement about how well they've done in such a short period of time. And then I've quietly said, 'You can do this. Why don't we have another try?'

We exalt parenting above almost any other role. When we fail to demonstrate perfection in our parenting, we feel a bit like that four-year-old who fell off her bike and skinned her knee. It hurts. It makes us question our ability. We wonder whether we're doing it right and whether we'll ever really get a handle on it.

None of us has ever really 'got this' when it comes to our parenting. We're all making it up as we go along. And while some of us may have read more books, had more children or gained more experience, none of us is ever going to get everything all 'right'. It's the same with being a spouse or partner, doing the work we are employed to do or even being ourselves. It's a struggle. And I believe it's meant to be. It teaches us to be better people.

Being a parent is tricky. It's tough. It's exhausting. But you can do this. The fact that you've read this book indicates you've got everything it takes to do it, and to do it well. While the book may be helpful, it's what's in your heart that matters most – and reading this book shows you care enough to make this work.

So let go a little and sit back, smile more and watch your precious children grow. Enjoy the small moments. Spend time together. Be there at the crossroads, do things together and teach them.

But most of all, love them – and show them every day.

Resources

In Chapter 1: Parenting on the Same Page, I describe the need for couples to 'get along'. Here are some resources that might be useful if things are challenging in your relationship:

21 Days to a Happier Family by Justin Coulson
Take Back Your Marriage by William J. Doherty
The Relationship Cure by John Gottman
The 7 Principles for Making Marriage Work by John Gottman
How to Improve Your Marriage Without Talking About It
     by Patricia Love and Steven Stosny
Authentic Happiness by Martin Seligman

For something a little heavier and more academic:
Reconcilable Differences by Andrew Christensen and Neil Jacobson

If you're open to reading a book with explicit Christian ideas try:
The Love Dare by Alex and Stephen Kendrick

Endnotes

In an effort to minimise the reader's need to look at inaccessible and expensive original academic sources in peer-reviewed journals, wherever possible I have referred, instead, to popular books on the relevant topics. Each of these books contains fascinating reading and deeply intensive research sources aligned with those I have used. For readers who wish to obtain specific details on the peer-reviewed, published studies upon which ideas in this book are based (if those articles are not already referenced below), please contact the author at info@justincoulson.com.

Chapter 1

Dr John Gottman …: this estimate is based on Gottman's research with couples in the United States. He details this research simply and clearly in his book, *The 7 Principles for Making Marriage Work*.

It's hard to shift habits …: for more on habits, see *The Power of Habit* by Charles Duhigg or *Willpower* by Roy Baumeister.

Ironically, Gottman has shown …: *The 7 Principles for Making Marriage Work* by Dr John Gottman.

Acceptance and enjoyment are the best fertilisers …: *Mindfulness, Acceptance, and Positive Psychology*. Edited by Todd Kashdan and Joseph Ciarrochi. See also *Meanings of Life* by Roy Baumeister.

It would be easy to focus …: ideas for activities throughout this book are primarily based on the foundational underpinnings of Appreciative Inquiry. The central figure in Appreciate Inquiry research is David Cooperrider, and while much of his work is done in corporate settings, it is broadly applicable in other contexts, including the family.

Chapter 2

Children whose parents …: this statement is based on decades of research in
   attachment theory. Modern updates to the theory are well-explained
   in the following three sources:
   Sroufe, A. & Siegel, D. (DATE) 'The verdict is in: The case for attachment
   theory.'; Schore, A. (2017). 'Modern attachment theory', in APA's
   Handbook of Trauma Psychology, p. 6; Schore, A. (2017). 'Modern
   attachment theory', in APA's Handbook of Trauma Psychology: Vol 1.

Researchers have found …: ibid.

A special note for dads …: There is an increasingly deep research-body on which
   we can draw for empirical work into the importance of fathers. However,
   in the interests of accessibility, see *Do Fathers Matter* by Paul Raeburn
   for a thorough synthesis of the research in a popular book format.
   See also *Gender and Parenthood* edited by Bradford Wilcox and Kathleen
   Kline (quite an academic treatment of the value of both parents for different
   reasons, from biological and social scientific perspectives). See also an
   article published in the Atlantic on 14 June 2013 by Bradford Wilcox,
   'The distinct, positive impact of a good dad': https://www.theatlantic.com/
   sexes/archive/2013/06/the-distinct-positive-impact-of-a-good-dad/276874/

Studies have shown that dads play a crucial role in guiding their children's
   development …:
   http://www.pewsocialtrends.org/files/2011/06/fathers-FINAL-report.pdf
   Lareau, A. (2000). 'My wife can tell me who I know: Methodological
   and conceptual problems in studying fathers.' *Qualitative Sociology*, 23,
   407–433.
   Brotherson, S. E., & White, J. M. (2007). *Why Fathers Count*. Men's studies
   press. Tennessee.

And in many cases, they do things mums typically don't do…:
   Raeburn, P. (2014). *Do Fathers Matter? What Science is Telling Us About the
   Parent We've Overlooked*. New York: Scientific American.

They get excited about physical prowess …:

> http://www.pewsocialtrends.org/files/2011/06/fathers-FINAL-report.pdf
> Lareau, A. (2000). 'My wife can tell me who I know: Methodological and conceptual problems in studying fathers.' *Qualitative Sociology, 23*, 407–433.
> Brotherson, S. E., & White, J. M. (2007). *Why Fathers Count.* Men's studies press. Tennessee.

Multiple studies, such as the one conducted by David Popenoe of Rutgers University …: Popenoe, D. (1996). *Life Without Father: Compelling new evidence that fatherhood and marriage are indispensable for the good of children and society.* New York: Free Press (page 147).

A bunch of simple studies …: see Sroufe and Schore references cited previously.

Research with adolescents …: this statement is supported by Australian research described here: https://link.springer.com/article/10.1007/s10826-016-0512-8 and is contrasted with this study here: https://www.ncbi.nlm.nih.gov/pmc/articles/PMC4373649/.

Respond actively and constructively …: Gable, S. L., Reis, H. T., Impett, E. A., & Asher, E. R. (2004). 'What do you do when things go right? The intrapersonal and interpersonal benefits of sharing positive events.' *Journal of Personality and Social Psychology, 87*, 228–245.

Phenomenon called mattering …: see Elliott, G. C., Kao, S., & Grant, A-M. (2004). 'Mattering: Empirical validation of a social-psychological concept.' *Self & Identity, 3*, 339–354.

Chapter 3

Regardless of the behaviour …: see *Self-Determination Theory* (2017) by Richard M Ryan and Edward L Deci.

Developmental researchers have …: see Wellman, H. M. (2017). 'The development of theory of mind: Historical reflections.' *Child Development Perspectives.* DOI: 10.1111/cdep.12236. See also the work of Slaughter, V. (2015). 'Theory of mind in infants and young children: A review.' *Australian Psychologist, 50*, 169–172.

In fact, people with power ...: Kraus, M. W., Cote, S., & Keltner, D. (2010). 'Social class, contextualism, and empathic accuracy.' *Psychological Science, 21.*

The late Dr Stephen Covey ...: in *The 7 Habits of Highly Effective People*

Big emotions often bring ...: this is based on the work of Barbra Fredrikson and the Broaden and Build Theory of Positive Emotions.

It's also critical to note ...: Nielsen, M., Haun, D., Kartner, J., & Legare, C. H. (2017). 'The persistent sampling bias in developmental psychology.' *Journal of Experimental Child Psychology, 162,* 31-38.

Chapter 4

There's always a well-known ...: H. L. Mencken as suggested at https://quoteinvestigator.com/2016/07/17/solution/

Marshall Rosenberg ...: Rosenberg, M. B. (2003) *Non-Violent Communication.*

Chapter 5

Ben and Jay ...: story used with permission.

Bullying that occurs between siblings ...: Bowes, L., Wolke, D., Joinson, C., Lereya, S. T., & Lewis, G. (2014). 'Sibling bullying and risk of depression, anxiety, and self-harm: A prospective cohort study.' *Pediatrics, 134,* e1032–e1039; DOI: 10.1542/peds.2014-0832. See also Wolke, D. and Samara, M. M. (2004), 'Bullied by siblings: association with peer victimisation and behaviour problems in Israeli lower secondary school children.' *Journal of Child Psychology and Psychiatry, 45,* 1015–1029. DOI:10.1111/j.1469-7610.2004.t01-1-00293.x

'After long arguments we often found ourselves ...': the quote comes from Wright, W., & Wright, O. (2004). *The published writings of Wilbur and Orville Wright*, edited by P. L. Jakab and R. Young. Washinton DC: Smithsonian Books.

Parents are the ones who start 75 per cent of fights with children ...: data presented by Dr John Gottman at Global HR Forum 2014, retrieved from Youtube on 20 May 2015: https://www.youtube.com/watch?v=dUE0kaQnQoo

Chapter 6

Money does not make us happier ...: this seems to be a startling revelation to many people. There are countless studies I could point to, but since most readers of these notes will be less concerned with reading peer-reviewed scholarly journal articles, my preference is to direct readers to books like *Happier* by Tal Ben-Shahar, *Authentic Happiness* by Martin Seligman, *The Happiness Hypothesis* by Jonathan Haidt or *The How of Happiness* by Sonja Lyubomirsky. Any popular evidence-based psychology book by a reputable researcher since around the late 1990s will confirm the strength of this research (with minimal, but occasional, caveats).

Chapter 7

Television is still a concern ...: the best review of the research in this area is found here: 'Children and Adolescents and Digital Media' by Yolanda (Linda) Reid Chassiakos, Jenny Radesky, Dimitri Christakis, Megan A. Moreno, Corinn Cross and COUNCIL ON COMMUNICATIONS AND MEDIA. Published in *Pediatrics* 2016;138. DOI: 10.1542/peds.2016-2593, originally published online 21 October 2016.

The best evidence from ...: The American Academy of Pediatrics policy statement and other research related to these guidelines are found here: http://pediatrics.aappublications.org/content/140/Supplement_2, accessed 2 November 2017

See also: https://www.aap.org/en-us/advocacy-and-policy/aap-health-initiatives/Pages/Media-and-Children.aspx.

As a counter, the Canadian policy statement offers minor differences: http://www.cps.ca/en/documents/position/screen-time-and-young-children.

The American Optometric Association ...: guidelines can be found here: https://www.aoa.org/patients-and-public/caring-for-your-vision/protecting-your-vision/computer-vision-syndrome?sso=y

For children in kindergarten ...: see this link: https://nces.ed.gov/ecls/kindergarten2011.asp, accessed 3 November 2017

Children eat about 170 calories more …: see this link: https://www.seattletimes.
com/opinion/smarter-kids-through-television-debunking-myths-old-and-
new/, accessed 3 November 2017

Compulsive Internet Use Scale:

Meerkerk, G.-J., Van Den Eijnden, R. J. J. M., Vermulst, A. A., &
Garretsen, H. F. L. (2009). 'The Compulsive Internet Use Scale (CIUS):
some psychometric properties.' *Cyberpsychology & Behavior, 12(1)*, 1–6.
More information on the psychometric properties of the Compulsive
Internet Use Scale, see this link: https://www.ncbi.nlm.nih.gov/
pubmed/19072079.

Conversely, reading fiction improves empathy …: according to several studies,
including those of Kidd and Castano in 2013, at The New School, NYC,
and Keith Oatley in 2016, at the University of Toronto:

Kidd, D. C., & Castano, E. (2013). 'Reading literary fiction improves
theory of mind.' *Science,* DOI: 10.1126/science.1239918

Damage to the insula …: Lin, Fuchun, Yan Zhou, Yasong Du, Lindi Qin,
Zhimin Zhao, Jianrong Xu, and Hao Lei (2012). 'Abnormal White Matter
Integrity in Adolescents with Internet Addiction Disorder: A Tract-Based
Spatial Statistics Study.' *PLOS ONE 7*, no. 1: e30253. DOI:10.1371/
journal.pone.0030253.

Other studies to support claims made in these paragraphs include:
Weng, Chuan-Bo, Ruo-Bing Qian, Xian-Ming Fu, Bin Lin, Xiao-Peng
Han, Chao-Shi Niu, and Ye-Han Wang. (August 2013) 'Gray Matter and
White Matter Abnormalities in Online Game Addiction.' *European Journal
of Radiology 82*, no. 8: 1308–1312. DOI:10.1016/j.ejrad.2013.01.031.
Yuan, Kai, Ping Cheng, Tao Dong, Yanzhi Bi, Lihong Xing, Dahua Yu,
Limei Zhao, et al. (January 9, 2013) 'Cortical Thickness Abnormalities
in Late Adolescence with Online Gaming Addiction.' Edited by
Bogdan Draganski. *PLOS ONE 8*, no. 1: e53055. DOI:10.1371/journal.
pone.0053055.

More information in an accessible and readable form is available at Victoria Dunckley's *Psychology Today* blog: https://www.psychologytoday.com/blog/mental-wealth/201402/gray-matters-too-much-screen-time-damages-the-brain

Cal Newport …: as stated in Newport, C. (2016). *Deep work*. Piatkus: New York.

Chapter 8

Australian researchers, Amanda Mergler …: this research and other interesting issues are summarised in this article on *The Conversation* website: https://theconversation.com/when-to-send-a-child-to-school-causes-anxiety-and-confusion-for-parents-81330 (accessed 24 July 2017).

Studies show that in the long run, children who learn …: while it's American-based and refers to their 'common core' standards, the ages and requirements described are suitable for describing precisely what I'm discussing. The most accessible summary for non-academics is found in this YouTube video: https://www.youtube.com/watch?v=DVVln1WMz0g&app=desktop where Professor Nancy Carlsson, a Doctor of Education at Lesley University, is quoted as pointing out this very issue.

New Zealand's Dr Sebastian …: see this link: http://www.otago.ac.nz/news/news/otago006408.html

US education expert, Alfie Kohn …: Kohn, A. (1992) *No contest. The case against competition*. Houghton Mifflin: New York.

Chapter 9

I heard in a conference …: Oaks, D. (2007). *Good, Better, Best*. Intellectual Reserve: Utah.

Acknowledgements

There is no role in life that matters more than 'parent'. Because of this, I take the responsibility of writing a book on parenting very seriously. I have been blessed to have extraordinary people around me to support me, guide me, inspire me and encourage me as this book came together.

Many of the ideas in this book emerged from, and were refined during, discussions with the most generous, kind and wise man I know: Professor H. Wallace Goddard. Over the past 15 years, Wally has been a mentor to me. In more recent years, he has become a sincere and joyous friend. Wally's fingerprints are on almost every page of this book, and I am deeply grateful for the time we've spent together talking, playing with ideas, learning and exploring. I acknowledge and appreciate the sacrifice of time and the investment of knowledge that Wally has given me. Gratitude also to Nancy, Wally's wife, who sacrificed precious time with him so we could work on these ideas. A huge thanks to Andy and Natalie Goddard, too, for allowing me a week's retreat in their home to focus solely on writing this book.

In Australia, Maggie Dent is a lighthouse for parents. Her common-sense wisdom and pragmatism, and her generous compassion for parents, make her endlessly popular. I appreciate Maggie's support and encouragement, and am especially grateful for her generosity in providing a foreword for this book.

I appreciate Professor Gert-Jan Meerkerk for allowing the use of the Compulsive Internet Use Scale. Professor Marc Brackett, Kathryn Lee and Robin Stern at the Yale Center for Emotional Intelligence kindly contributed to this book. Their input is genuinely appreciated and will be beneficial for every parent who reads their words.

The team at ABC Books are a pleasure to work with and I am grateful for Katie Stackhouse and Barbara McClenahan; their gentle and wise guidance makes my writing far more enjoyable to read. It was also a delight to work with Kate

O'Donnell again. Everything Kate touches is improved with her expert eye, and I'm thankful for her attention to detail and thoughtful insight.

Incredible people have had conversations with me (or written me emails or shared links or blog posts) that have sparked ideas for this book and I acknowledge them: Steve Biddulph, Michael Grose, Jodie Benveniste, Bruce Sullivan, Dr Paula Robinson, Dr Philip Tam, Alfie Kohn, Gert-Jan Meerkerk and Dr Marc Brackett and team. Countless parents, teachers, school principals, wellbeing coordinators, counsellors and conference participants – as well as Facebook and blog readers – have also prompted crucial ideas or supplied stories and examples that have been used here, and I recognise and thank them for their input. I also appreciate those who reviewed (and provided endorsements for) the book. Thank you.

And I'm immensely grateful for my team. As I wrote this book, I was blessed with outstanding support from Andrea Coorey, Evelynne Hatchard, Sasha Dumaresq and Stacey Packer. I feel fortunate to have been able to work with such committed, passionate and kind people. Andrea, your insights, attention to detail and care have been a wonderful asset to my work. I appreciate our relationship. Evelynne, you're an artist! You make my work *look* next level and more. Sasha ... wow! Energiser bunny. Thanks for plugging gaps and being so in, even when you didn't know if you could. And Stacey, thanks for helping me carve out the time and space to do what matters most when it matters most.

As always, family must be acknowledged. I was raised by a mum and dad who always made me feel like I matter. This may be the greatest gift that they have given me. I'm grateful to them for their unqualified and unconditional support. I love you both. Same goes for Alisa, Karina, Tim, Rachel and Leah. Love you, fam.

My kids. Wow. What can I say? I'm crazy about them. I'm so blessed to have them. Chanel, Abbie, Ella, Annie, Lilli and Emilie. You're the reason I do what I do. You're the reason I wrote this book. I hope I can live up to the standard you're worthy of.

Finally, my wife, helpmeet and eternal companion, Kylie. I couldn't do this without you. I wouldn't want to. For your endless support, thank you.

Index

Also by Dr Justin Coulson

21
Days
to a Happier
Family

Parenting expert Dr Justin Coulson knows how to make families happier! *21 Days to a Happier Family* combines cutting-edge insights from positive psychology with classic psychological research to help parents identify and develop habits that will strengthen their family. In his trademark warm and empathic style, Dr Coulson covers topics such as finding the most effective parenting style for your child, getting relationships right and how that leads to effective discipline, using mindfulness in parenting, being emotionally available to your children – and so much more.

'Parenthood can be a jungle, but Justin's advice and simple strategies will help you find that path back to sanity, stability and smiling kids.'
Lisa Wilkinson

'Justin Coulson's compassionate and helpful advice helps me unravel my many parenting dilemmas.'
Jessica Rowe

Also by Dr Justin Coulson

9
Ways
to a Resilient
Child

9 Ways to a Resilient Child gives parents practical strategies to help their children cope with the challenges that life throws at them – from friendship problems and bullying to losing a game or failing an exam. Even our home environment and the way that we parent can impact our children's potential to recover from difficulty.

Dr Justin Coulson explains the factors that help or hinder resilience and why common advice such as 'Toughen up, Princess' just doesn't work. Learn the psychological secrets that will build your child's capacity to bounce back, stronger and more resilient than ever, including the ability to think flexibly, exercise self-control, and make safe and healthy choices. Discover the powerful impact of family, relationships, school and community, and the most effective ways to support your child.

'Justin Coulson explains clear strategies designed to
help parents embody optimism and compassion as they
guide their children through the unpredictable journey
of growing up in a very complex world.'
Dr Diana Korevaar – Author of *Mindfulness
for Mums and Dads*